D1194943

AWAKEN

the

SLEEPING GIANT

CRAIG KOLAVO

DEDICATION

I dedicate this book to my kids, Samantha and Clayton.
I hope that by sharing some of my discoveries from this
amazing adventure, their journey might be made a little
easier. And to my wife, Amy. I am grateful for your daily
dose of love, support, and inspiration.

WATER.ORG

All e-book proceeds will benefit this amazing organization. Founded over twenty-five years ago by Matt Damon and Gary White, water.org has made it their mission to bring safe water and sanitation solutions to the world. This dedicated group has empowered the lives of nearly 30 million people with their innovative ideas related to the global water crisis.

When I first researched this organization, I was reminded of a quote from the Chinese philosopher Lao Tzu. "Give a man a fish and you feed him for a day. Teach a man to fish and you feed him for a lifetime." Charity alone is not a long-term solution. By providing small affordable loans and many other expert resources, water.org has helped millions of people discover something most of us take for granted: access to running water and a toilet.

These basic provisions create conditions for improved health, privacy, and safety. This can be life-changing for those in need. All human beings deserve this simple dignity. Thank you for joining me on this heroic mission.

— CRAIG KOLAVO

CONTENTS

INTRODUCTION

My original intention for writing this book was simple and somewhat selfish. I was hoping to explain to *my* children some of the discoveries I've made on this crazy adventure of life. Maybe all parents feel this way at some point. Why should my kids have to experience the same struggles, pain, and suffering I've been through? I know stuff! They can learn from my mistakes.

Organizing boxes of journals and notes into a coherent story was a monumental task that proved to be a painfully slow process. Months turned into years. Finally, I stepped back and began to see the story unfolding before me. This writing process was surprisingly transformational. It was like I'd discovered a secret treasure map. Unfortunately, this map was given to me in puzzle form, and the pieces were revealed over decades. Funny how the Universe works.

When this puzzle was finally assembled, it was a real *aha* moment. On second thought, it was actually more of an *oh-shit* moment! Although I was excited to see on paper what I'd been feeling for many years, the thought of sharing my ideas was terrifying. My insecurities quickly came to the surface. My demons were saying, "Who the hell do you think you are? People will think you're crazy!" I'm grateful for my wife and the small group of friends who motivated me throughout this painstaking process.

As I studied the treasure map, a theme began to emerge. Through my decades of soul-searching, the same nagging questions kept bubbling to the surface. Why is there so much pain and suffering in this world? Why are so many of us living with illness, disease, and addiction? Why all the fear, anxiety, and hate? The entire planet seems to be on edge, and temperatures are rising.

By stepping back and taking a panoramic view of the situation, the answers began to reveal themselves. It became obvious to me that we continue to repeat the same mistakes. We are treating the symptoms of our disease, which is the chaos we see in our world, rather than exploring for the root cause. Focusing on symptoms will only result in prescriptions for bigger bombs and more Prozac.

Instead, why don't we ask the difficult questions, like "Why is everyone so pissed off?" Contrary to what many believe, this worldwide crisis did not start on September 11, 2001, nor did it begin on November 8th, 2016. We have been sleepwalking for generations. We've been stuck in a depressive state of apathy, allowing a loud minority to rule the often-silent majority. The struggles we see in the outer world are a direct reflection of the battle being played out in our inner world. We have been consumed by the external stimuli, completely identified with our small selves.

In other words, we have been disconnected from our True Nature. This is the "root cause" I'm referring to. Most of life's pain, suffering, and struggles can be traced back to this disconnection. When we learn how to end this inner battle, peace will soon follow in the outer world.

Despite these turbulent times, I am still an optimist. I feel we are entering a stage of positive change and increased awareness. Unfortunately, it's often darkest before the dawn. **It's time for a revolution**! A simple shift in awareness is all that is needed for this spiritual revolution. No shots will be fired, and no blood will be shed. It is time to rediscover our Primal Way.

Although this book is not about religion or politics, we will soon discover this shift can supercharge any religious practice and will inspire us to demand more from our leaders. Inspire us to become leaders! A Sleeping Giant lies dormant within all of us. **It's time for a wakeup call!** This is your birthright. You were born into royalty. Reclaim your power and join the revolution.

As I will explain, to *forget* our Divine Nature is a necessary stage in the Game of Life, but so is *remembering!* As human beings on this amazing adventure, we all share the same primal purpose: to **Discover** our Divine Nature, to **Surrender** to this power within, and to **Inspire** others on this journey. This is the spiritual path in a nutshell.

In the chapters that follow, I will discuss the six stages of life we all will *eventually* experience.

1. **Alien Birth**: Our journey begins at birth, when we all get delivered into this strange world as a Soul with a Body. We are transitioning from a world of pure Spirit to the world of form. I can only imagine how frightening this must be for the newborn opening her eyes for the first time and seeing all the strange faces staring back. Feeling like an alien on a strange planet, we soon discover primal fear. This fear quickly leads to the creation of our Bodyguard. This is a survival instinct. Your loyal Bodyguard will accompany you for a very long time on this journey.

2. **The School of Life**: Shortly after birth, we will all enter the School of Life. No time to waste. We need to learn the ropes. To become street-smart, we must explore Human Nature and learn how to play the Game. The Soul

is not required for this part of the journey, so this Giant will sleep for now. As a matter of fact, we become so accustomed to taking instructions from our Bodyguard that we completely forget our Sleeping Giant. Have no shame. This temporary amnesia is all part of the plan. The School of Life will repeatedly attempt to lead us back to our True Selves.

3. **Discovery**: Eventually, we will all rediscover the Sleeping Giant. The lessons learned throughout the School of Life will finally inspire us to look within. When the Giant awakens, he will be ready to reclaim the throne. This is an exciting time. Unfortunately, the Bodyguard will not be ready to step aside.

4. **Epic Battle**: The stage is now set for an Epic Battle. The Giant and the Bodyguard will fight for control. Since man cannot serve two masters, we find ourselves torn. Although we are excited to reunite with our Soul, we also feel a sense of loyalty to our longtime friend, the Bodyguard. We cannot evolve on this journey until this Battle comes to a peaceful conclusion. We are often stuck in this stage for ages. When the Bodyguard finds the strength and courage to Surrender, a blissful merger will follow.

5. **Surrender**: All experiences in life are intended to lead us to this moment. For the lucky few who make it to this stage, the struggles of life come to an end. When Body and Soul reunite as one, you will be transformed. When the dust settles, you will discover you've become a <u>Super</u>natural <u>Hu</u>man. You now get to live the rest of your life as Super-Man on a heroic mission. This is where the magic begins!

6. **Inspire**: This is the fun part! The tests, trials, and struggles are over. You have traveled full circle. You will find yourself exactly where you are needed most. You will now get to choose how to carry out your mission. You will discover hidden powers and secrets will be revealed. You will lead by example and Inspire others on this grand adventure. Service now becomes your passion.

During this adventure, you will get to know Buddy and friends. The Monkey, the Bodyguard, and the Giant all play pivotal roles during these six stages of development.

Body Guard   **Buddy**   **Monkey**   **Giant**

Throughout the book, I will also explore some important questions: Why do we resist *Surrender*? Why does the *Epic Battle* seem to be never ending? Why do we remain stuck in the *School of Life* for so long if this "unconscious" stage was only intended to be temporary? What the hell has happened to us? When did we become so complacent, happy to chase temporary highs only to find ourselves lingering in a dull state of sadness? Have we settled on the old adage "Life's a bitch and then you die?" Have we become comfortable with our discomfort?

I must confess that one of the main reasons I was stuck for so long was simple laziness. It takes some effort to Soul-search and aspire to a more meaningful life.

Most of us won't make this effort until the pain becomes unbearable. This is the School of Life doing its job. If we continue to make the same mistakes, the lessons will become more painful. This is a Universal Law that cannot be avoided. Unfortunately, many of us will need to hit rock bottom before we decide to look within for answers. In this respect, pain is good. Without this Universal Law at work in the world, we would never evolve.

I have a theory of why this natural evolutionary process feels so painfully slow, even after we hit that unacceptable level of misery. When we finally begin to look for answers, our spiritual teachers instruct us to start by killing the Bodyguard (i.e., Ego, Separate Self). This is very confusing since this loyal friend has been with us from the beginning. In addition, we are often directed to study our cherished religious texts, such as the Bible, the Torah, the Quran, the Vedas, the Sutras and others. These amazing books are packed with wisdom, but they can be very difficult to understand. Most were written thousands of years ago in ancient languages. Even the scholars argue over their translations. To make matters worse, they are loaded with parables and metaphors that are also open to many different interpretations. Before the invention of the printing press in the 1400s, these books were copied by hand. Many experts have questioned the accuracy of these handwritten copies passed down over generations.

Whose translations are correct? Whose book is correct? We have been killing each other in the name of God for centuries over these questions. I don't think the spiritual path was intended to be so complicated.

Unfortunately, the Game of Life didn't come with a simple set of instructions. How are we supposed to be good at something without knowing the rules? In the following chapters, I will provide a clear message to simplify and demystify the spiritual path. This includes practical instructions that can be incorporated into your daily life immediately. Although we can't skip any of the steps on this adventure, I hope this book will shed some light on the path, so you might walk a little faster.

CHAPTER 1

ALIEN BIRTH

Our amazing adventure as human beings begins at birth, when we are delivered into this world as Body and Soul. Most descriptions of this event are told from the mother's or father's point of view. Have you ever tried to imagine what this experience must be like for the newborns? What do they see and feel? How frightening this must be!

Although none of us remember the birthing experience, I'm guessing it's similar to an alien crashing on a strange planet. To support this notion, I looked up the definition of *alien*. "Any being or thing foreign to the environment in which it now exists. An outsider belonging to a very different place. From another world." This is perfect! We are emerging from the safe, beautiful energy world of pure Spirit and are violently pulled into this world of form. No wonder most babies arrive screaming bloody murder.

Imagine experiencing all your bodily senses for the first time in this harsh environment of bright lights, loud noises, cold air, etc. To open your eyes and see all these strange creatures staring back at you–yikes! This is probably why God didn't give newborns the ability to walk. Hospitals would be full of babies trying to escape.

I've witnessed childbirth twice. I know I'm supposed to say this was the most beautiful thing I've ever seen, but I'm sorry. It was frightening and looked like a crime scene when it was over. Welcome to planet Earth! This is how our journey begins.

I love this quote from Pierre Teilhard de Chardin, the Jesuit priest and philosopher (1881-1955): "We are Spiritual Beings having a human experience." This one sentence says so much. We are born into this world as a Soul with a Body. The Body is our physical self, temporary in nature, made up of flesh, bones, organs, brain, mind, etc. The Soul is our spiritual essence, the eternal part of our human form, often referred to as the *Higher Self.* We are born with the perfect combination of Human Nature and Divine Nature, both equally important for the Game that lies ahead.

Since our Soul exists in the invisible realm, our resources for understanding are strained. Our language and our 3-D minds limit our ability to grasp this concept of Soul. We still live in a world that says, "I'll believe it when I see it." I too was guilty of this limited thinking until I realized how much invisible stuff we commonly accept in our modern world. Consider cellular technology, radio waves, radar, and ultrasound, just to name a few. We all use invisible IR light technology (infrared) every time we pick up our TV remote control. We have faith in this invisible realm without understanding how it really works. Maybe it won't be such a huge leap of faith to accept the Soul as real, even though it won't show up in a selfie.

Science and technology have been catching up with beliefs the ancient yogis have had for ages. For example, everything in the universe is connected as vibrating energy. In other words, nothing is solid. Einstein said, "This is physics, not philosophy." Before the invention of the high-powered microscope, you would have been considered insane to believe such a thing. Today this is common knowledge. Although Nikola Tesla was not a yogi, he often collaborated with Swami Vivekananda. The

Swami was hoping to use science to explain the invisible energy field the Hindus have intuitively known about for centuries. He often said, "I see the perfect union between science and spirituality." Anyway, many of Tesla's ideas related to this invisible energy field were also considered crazy until science proved them to be true. The Dalai Lama has been collaborating with neuroscientist to prove the benefits of meditation to the world of doubters. In short, science continues to validate ideas that were previously considered outrageous.

Science can be a great truth teller, but don't let it be your only source of validation. As Ralph Waldo Emerson said, "All I have seen teaches me to trust the Creator for all I have not seen." If ancient cultures relied on science to shape their beliefs, they would have all passed from this world fearful and unsure of anything. Don't wait for science to prove something you inherently know is true! The spiritual path is guided by intuition, not intellect. All human beings are born with a Soul. If you are skeptical, I will ask that you suspend your disbelief for a few hours while reading this book. This will be necessary to tap into the amazing powers you will soon discover hidden within. I promise the results will be immediate. Results are my truth teller. What do you have to lose? If you finish the book and think it's all a bunch of crap, at least you were open-minded enough to try. One thing I know for sure, it's a hell of a lot more fun to be open-minded, living in a world of infinite possibilities.

I believe that as young children, we are still aware of both realms. We are coming from an energy world of Spirit, a safe place where we feel the pure love of being connected to our Source. We are also becoming conscious of this strange new world of form. Every moment is a grand exploration. Our natural instinct is to connect with like energy. Although our parents and family may have had good intentions, as infants we did not recognize them as being the same as us. Their energy felt different. Sorry, mom ☹.

Remember, we were recently plucked from the world of Spirit, which can only be explained as the high vibration of pure love. In this moment, this is all we know. We are innocent, trusting, unworldly beings not yet corrupted by this strange new world.

To make the situation more challenging, we do not yet identify with our bodies. What a mess! Stuck in the middle. One foot still clinging to the world of Spirit and one foot in your mouth. It's funny, but true. Have you watched infants discovering their bodies? They stare at their hands and feet with curiosity and amazement as if these body parts were separate from themselves. Not until we try eating our fingers and toes will we discover our oneness with this body. It's really amazing how quickly we adapt from the world of Spirit to the world of form.

Okay, so we find ourselves on this alien planet, living in this strange body. We are surrounded by all these large alien beings who seem to be hovering over us 24/7. Now what?

Sometime during early development, we will all experience *primal fear*. This occurs the first moment we feel alone. It doesn't matter how loving and caring those around you might be. There is no comparison to that world of pure Spirit. Maybe infants cry because they still remember where they came from and they are longing for home. Who can blame them? This primal fear is a good thing. Our survival instincts will kick in for the first time. We begin to focus all our attention on the physical world around us, and this strange form we find ourselves inhabiting. I now have a body, a brain, and a mind. I must quickly learn how to use it! We have people to please, tricks to learn, and love to earn. Not wanting to risk exposing our True Self, an alien in this strange new world, we quickly learn how to play the Game. We imitate those around us to feel safe. Our minds create this persona, mask, or *separate self* as a means of protection. This separate self becomes our Bodyguard.

With all of our attention focused on surviving in this physical world, our Divine Nature soon takes a backseat to our Human Nature. The Soul, our only connection to the Divine, agrees to step aside. Man cannot serve two masters, and we have much to learn about Human Nature. The Soul will fall into a deep sleep for now.

Everything described above is a necessary part of God's Game Plan. No mistakes. Nothing to feel guilty about. To forget our Divine Nature is necessary for human development. We did not have a choice. This is a natural part of our spiritual evolution. This human experience will soon become the School of Life. We cannot expect to succeed in School if we are homesick every day. To "forget" was necessary to fully commit to this strange new world. The Sleeping Giant (Soul) will eventually awaken to play a very big role in this amazing adventure.

As a child, the Bodyguard is very important. He is a quick learner and will try to protect us from both physical and emotional harm. We learn the easiest way to blend in is to mimic those around us. This is why our environment plays such a big role in these early stages, when we are developing the ego and personality.

In the beginning, we are aware of the mask that we are hiding behind. We are very protective of our vulnerable Soul. However, as time passes, we forget about our True Self, the Sleeping Giant. We begin to believe that this mind-made character we have created is the "real me." Again, this is all part of the Game Plan. Everything is unfolding perfectly. Your loyal Bodyguard has good intentions and will do his best to protect you on this journey. The stage is now set to enter the School of Life.

SUMMARY

As we transition from the world of Spirit to the world of form, we find ourselves in a very strange place. As spiritual beings having this human experience, we feel fear for the first time. This *primal fear* leads to the creation of the *Bodyguard*, who will become our loyal partner for years to come. Our True Self must step aside for this portion of our adventure. This *Sleeping Giant* will soon become a distant memory. This temporary amnesia is necessary during this phase of our journey. The Sleeping Giant will awaken when the time is right. For now, we have much to learn.

CHAPTER 2

THE SCHOOL OF LIFE

The School of Life is meant to teach us about Human Nature and to prepare us for our heroic mission. Again, "We are spiritual beings having a human experience." We have much to learn, and our survival depends on it. Another popular quote that resonates with me is "I am in this world, but not of this world." Both share a similar meaning. We are in a strange new world having an experience that is foreign to us. The School of Life is the first step on our journey.

This process is actually the same for any new adventure. What if you were born and raised in New York City and accepted a job transfer to Peru? You will quickly discover upon your arrival that you have much to learn. Living in a foreign land, you not only need to learn the basics (language, currency, diet, climate, etc.), but you will also need to become street-smart. To accomplish this, you must immerse yourself into the culture. Learning local slang, rituals, traditions, and taboos can be just as important for survival. Through trial and error, you will learn many lessons. This is also true for the School of Life. This is so much more than an intellectual journey. This School is an experiential adventure.

As I mentioned in the introduction, I believe we all share the same primal purpose which is to Discover, Surrender and Inspire. Consider the School of Life as a prerequisite for this journey. Before we can earn this gift of awareness, we must complete our schooling. We must live through the highs and lows of the human experience. Although some of these lessons can be painful, they are all necessary to fulfill our purpose and become effective leaders. As I will discuss in future chapters, learning compassion, unconditional love, and forgiveness can be some of the most challenging lessons. Unfortunately, we cannot move forward until we embody these spiritual virtues into our human experience.

Before we continue, I would like to revisit a principle that is very important but often misunderstood. We are unconscious during this stage of life. **It is necessary for us to temporarily forget our true identity**. I have heard many spiritual teachers suggest that forgetting our Divine Nature is the root of all evil. I strongly disagree with this notion!

I feel this belief is responsible for why so many of us remain stuck our entire lives. Creating a stigma of shame and guilt will only delay our evolution. This faulty concept also creates a sense of despair. *It's too late for me. I have turned my back on God for too long.* How can we be held responsible for something that naturally occurs to all of us shortly after we arrive on this planet?

As we evolve on this path, we will develop self-awareness. Until then, have no shame. God doesn't make mistakes. If you are skeptical, consider the alternative. After you are born, you do *not* forget. As a child, you remain fully aware of your Divine Self. As one of these rare enlightened children, why would you ever choose to go out into this scary world to learn about the human experience? You would probably lock yourself in your room and pray to return home ASAP. When you complete your lessons in the School of Life, your temporary amnesia will be lifted, and you will be ready to reclaim your power. For now, the Giant sleeps. You have been sent away to School, and God will patiently wait for your return. Yes, eventually we will all remember and reunite with the Divine within.

Since the School of Life is an unconscious stage, you might ask, "Why waste my time discussing something I have no control over?" This is a fair question. I am honestly not sure if sharing the ideas in this book could really make a difference to those who are currently working through this stage. After all, you won't become a *seeker* until the

Sleeping Giant awakens. You will have no interest in self-discovery, and you would never voluntarily read a book about the spiritual path. Since hindsight is such a great teacher, I will tell you my experience and let you decide. The Universe works in mysterious ways.

When I was about thirty years old, people who were "seekers" began showing up in my life. Although I thought they were kind of weird, they seemed to be happier than most, as if they had a secret. I was intrigued. I remember calling one of my new friends to join me for dinner one evening. She said yes but had a meeting to attend first. She invited me to join her. I was lured by the promise of snacks and cocktails. The meeting was with a study group to discuss a book called *A Course in Miracles.* Although I thought these discussions were very strange, I hung out and enjoyed a few adult beverages before going to dinner.

About a month later, I spent the weekend at a friend's house in Houston. On Sunday morning, I was invited to go to a church service. I laughed and explained that I was not a religious guy. I was told not to worry because this was not a traditional church, and it would be fun. Since the football game I planned to watch didn't start until 3 p.m., I went along for the ride and discovered Unity Church. I must admit, it was pretty cool. It was a casual, nondenominational gathering with a very positive, uplifting message.

After the service, I noticed a poster advertising an upcoming event with Wayne Dyer as the keynote speaker. I recognized Wayne's name because I had read his book *Pulling Your Own Strings* when I was in college. I really liked this book. Back in the 1970s and 1980s, Wayne wrote several powerful self-help books. I also saw him on *The Tonight Show* a couple of times. He was a very inspirational character. I quickly went into the Unity bookstore and purchased a ticket. I thought it was odd that this celebrity author would be making an appearance at a church, but my curiosity was overwhelming.

To my surprise, Wayne had evolved over the years. He transformed himself from being a self-help motivational author into a spiritual guru. I enjoyed the event but wondered if I didn't like the old version of Wayne better. It was a little awkward for me. I thought he used the *G-word* too much, and I couldn't really grasp many of the ideas he discussed. I followed the mob of people afterward to purchase a couple of his latest books and left feeling a little disappointed. The books sat in my nightstand untouched for over a year. I was obviously not ready.

All three of these experiences happened within a two-month period (*A Course in Miracles* study group, Unity Church service, and the Wayne Dyer lecture). If I had been more aware at the time, I would have felt the Universe guiding me. Unfortunately, I was still clueless.

Unable to sleep one night, I turned on my lamp and took out one of the books from my nightstand. Although I was skeptical, I was feeling worn down from the stress and drama unfolding in my daily life. I was curious and decided I had nothing to lose. To my surprise, I found the book to be very inspiring and was up most of the night reading.

The next day when I got home from work, I closed the mini blinds, locked the doors, put on some headphones, and tried to meditate for the first time. It was challenging at first, but I liked it. I would love to say there was a lightning bolt moment or some crazy vision, but no such luck!

I gradually started to feel different. I was more relaxed. My days became less of a struggle. In other words, I saw results. I now understand that my Higher Self had been patiently waiting for this opportunity. It was as if I unlocked the door and the Universe kicked it open. After this brief period of open-mindedness, books, people, and events began to *accidentally* show up in my life, gently nudging me toward this spiritual path. I didn't know what the hell was going on, but for the first time in my life, I felt like I was getting help from some invisible force. My feelings of *It's me against the world* began to diminish. Although I couldn't explain it at the time, I no longer felt alone. I was hooked! Unknowingly, I was becoming a *seeker* on my spiritual path.

I am telling this story while hoping to inspire those who are now experiencing the School of Life. Consider being open to new ideas, even if they seem weird at first. What do you have to lose? If someone gave you this book and you have no desire to read it, please don't throw it away. Put it in your nightstand. Maybe someday you will be inspired to pick it up again. A part of me hopes that on a subconscious level, I might be able to nudge the Sleeping Giant and help someone begin his or her awakening process.

If I'm preaching to the choir and you are already on this path, maybe you can be that *weird friend* who sparks the curiosity in someone else. Never miss a chance on this journey to inspire others. If you choose to be on a covert mission, secretly put this book into someone's mailbox. As I mentioned in the introduction, I feel a sense of urgency. There is too much dis-ease and conflict in the world. Too many of us are sleepwalking through life. We are in desperate need of an awakening on this planet now. Although I know we can't skip School, maybe by sharing what I've learned, I can help others graduate early.

The School of Life is the stage when we are dominated by our separate self a.k.a. the Bodyguard. When I say, "We are dominated," I am referring to our Human

Nature, which is made up of our body, brain, and mind. For future reference, I will use the acronym BBM when referring to the *physical* self. Okay, so the BBM is like an amazing supercomputer waiting for instructions. Like all computers, it needs to be programmed to function. During this stage of our evolution, the mind-made Bodyguard is our programmer. This training period is a very important part of our journey. All experiences during this period are stored in our memory. Our supercomputer has a massive hard drive (mind/consciousness).

Even though we are spiritually unconscious during our training, none of these experiences will go to waste. Everything happens for a reason. There is a Universal Law that says *all experiences in life are perfect and for our benefit.* Although this concept can be very difficult to accept during this stage, we will all eventually come to understand this truth. Memories of difficult and painful experiences that may haunt us during School will be of great benefit after awakening. As we evolve, we will discover that these painful lessons transform into wisdom. God is strengthening you for this adventure. What doesn't kill you makes you stronger. If it does kill you, you will get to return for another try.

Most of us spend eons stuck in this learning phase. How long we spend at each level is determined by *free will.* At this stage, we all experience some levels of joy and happiness, but also a lot of pain and suffering. I guess the *big* question might be "How long must I endure this stage of the Game? I am tired of these struggles! How do I advance to the next level?" Have you ever found yourself thinking, *What the hell is going on? Is life really supposed to be so difficult?*

Like any school, the School of Life will test you. All life experiences are learning lessons and the Universe is a powerful teacher. Some students will take the time to study each lesson and will advance quickly. Many others will race to the next experience without reflecting on the present moment. These students are too worried about future events to slow down and learn from the *now*. Unfortunately, this is how most of us live. As a result, we feel trapped in what seems to be a never-ending cycle of struggle.

Luckily, things will get worse. Seriously, this is not a typo. At first, the Universe will give us a gentle poke intended to guide us on the correct path. If we ignore this lesson, that gentle poke will get a little stronger. The longer we ignore these clues, the more painful the lessons will become. Eventually, it's like getting hit over the head with a club!

I spent a lot of time stuck in this phase. Yes, I was one of the stubborn ones. I've had plenty of lumps on my head! This is what I mean by "Luckily, things will get worse." Since all of life's experiences are meant to guide us, in hindsight, even the painful events should be considered blessings. If these lessons did not get progressively worse, you really would be stuck in a never-ending cycle with no hope for change.

Fortunately for us slow learners, the discomfort becomes so unbearable that we finally learn the lesson and make the necessary changes. The purpose of creation is for us to evolve. God does not want us to be stuck. The Universe wants us to succeed! Have you heard the saying, "The Universe works in mysterious ways"? Well, this stage is not very mysterious. Pay attention to all of life's experiences. Reflect on the results. If you don't like the results, adjust and move on. Avoid the club.

During the School of Life, our Human Nature always has us longing for more. This is all part of the Game Plan. We feel a void deep down inside. Something is missing. Since we are only aware of our physical world, we look to outside sources to help satisfy this empty feeling (more toys, money, food, sex, power, drugs, alcohol, etc.). Relief from these external sources is only temporary. As we go through this process, we discover the empty feelings remain.

I was caught in this trap of continuously striving for more. Unfortunately, most people in today's society look at this trait as a positive quality. We are considered to be type-A personalities. This might be an appropriate description if type-A stands for "asshole." I found there is often collateral damage during this *ambitious* stage of life. At some point, we will blame our jobs, friends, family, or spouse for our lack of fulfillment. Depression, divorce, drug and alcohol abuse, can all be a result of this dissatisfaction. *Maybe I can numb that empty feeling.*

Most of the world's population is in pain because we can't figure out how to *fill the void*. Like an itch we can't scratch. Satisfying this inherent craving becomes an unconscious life pursuit. Without the proper understanding, dissatisfaction continues to grow. External solutions might provide some temporary relief but only make matters worse in the long run, often leading to addiction and disease. The School of Life is everyone's first step, designed to lead us to Discovery.

Buddhist doctrine teaches that *all of life is suffering caused by our desires*. In a recent interview, the Dalai Lama offered some clarification of this teaching. He explained that all human beings have "desires." These desires are not necessarily bad. He suggested the word *dissatisfaction* might help us better understand this concept. All of life is suffering caused by our dissatisfaction. We desire something different because we are dissatisfied. Yes! This now makes sense to me. Over our lifetime, we have all accumulated a long list of preferences, *likes* and *dislikes*. Instead of enjoying the natural flow of life, most of us are trying to control this process by forcing life to align with our preferences. As a result, we spend our entire existence living in a state of anxiety, fear, and worry.

We are suffering for no reason. The spiritual path is simply *choosing* to go with the flow. The universe has been unfolding for 13.8 billion years. It will continue to unfold whether you like it or not, so why not *choose* to like it! Spiritual masters all appear to be calm and relaxed because they know this secret. As Jesus taught,

"My burden is light." We suffer because we strive for a *happy* life. We are taught as children that this should be the ultimate goal. Parents often say, "I just want my children to be happy." Talk about a heavy burden!

Although our teachers may have had good intentions, we have been misled. Since all emotions are fleeting, including happiness, this desire will only lead to more anxiety. Instead, I think it would be better if we focus on living a life of meaning. When you are living an inspired life (in-spirit), it doesn't really matter if you are happy every moment. To be content and at ease is the foundation of a meaningful life. This is the secret of the masters.

Before moving on, I think it is critical that we understand the Universal Law that states, "All of life's experiences happen for a reason and the Universe does not make mistakes." Call it *God's* Game Plan. To graduate from this School of Life, we must trust our Teacher. I understand this can be very difficult to swallow when you are in the middle of a terrible experience. How can [fill in the blank] be for my benefit (my drug addiction, breast cancer, job loss, car accident, abuse, etc.)? A lot of bad stuff can happen to us. I understand the anger, pain, and confusion. I have no desire to debate this idea with anyone. Emotions run too high when we are in the middle of the shit storm. I can only tell you what I have learned through my personal experiences.

In every adversity lie seeds of wisdom and grace. There are many ways to say it, but accepting this Universal Truth is a difficult but necessary part of our evolution. I promise, there is light at the end of the tunnel, but you can't bring the anger and hate with you. Clinging to this suffering will not change the past. It will only poison you and lead to disease. Why let the worst experiences of your life dictate your future? It is possible to make peace and accept this truth, even though you do not *yet* understand what benefit or wisdom will come. This is what it means to have *faith*.

At times, it will take years for these seeds of wisdom to bloom. Our first reaction is usually *Why me?* If we listen carefully, the answers will be revealed. I now understand that every experience in my life was necessary. All of it! Yes, the illnesses, injuries, failed relationships, addictions, etc. Every experience provided learning opportunities, and I would not trade one of these moments. Life's greatest lessons are often taught during our darkest hours.

I think we can all agree that the loss of a child might top the list of challenging life events. I have friends who lost their teenage son, Dan, to cancer. As I was writing this chapter, I asked Roger, Dan's father, if he would share his insights on this subject. I specifically asked what he thought about this "Universal Law" that says *everything happens for a reason and God does not make mistakes.* As you might imagine, I was anxious about making this phone call, not knowing how Roger felt about this concept. Roger's answer was sincere and courageous. I thank him for allowing me to use his experience to inspire others. Roger said,

> Although my faith was tested, and I lived through some anger after Dan's diagnosis, I soon came to believe that God had a plan for us. If taking Dan early was part of this plan, our family will be a tool to help others.

This was very powerful to hear. To have the courage to look for the hidden meaning in such a painful experience is amazing. Almost immediately following Dan's death, Roger and Dawn, his parents, founded an organization to support young adults struggling with cancer. Dan's House of Hope has touched the lives of thousands of families over the past several years. Their ten-year anniversary will be in 2020. Their life is now a heroic mission. Visit danshouseofhope.org to learn more.

Another story of triumph over adversity involves my friend Joanne "Fanny" Barry. Fanny was diagnosed with breast cancer fifteen years ago. After going through the treatments associated with this disease, Fanny not only survived but has thrived. I called Fanny as I was writing this chapter to hear her opinion on the School of Life. Fanny said,

> The learning lesson for me came during my cancer treatment. To be honest, I am still learning from it. I was always a believer that *everything in life happens for a reason* but felt that I knew what was best for me and I could force life to see things my way. Cancer taught me that being forceful was not the best way. Cancer humbled me. To find my way I had to either die or change. It would have been nice if I could have learned this without the cancer, but it seems like I needed a push, a helping hand. So perhaps cancer was my friend telling me if I don't change, I will miss the point of life. We all have life lessons. We are supposed to learn from these lessons and move on. Sometimes we make mistakes and that's okay, it's part of the process. It is the repetition of mistakes that lead to injury or illness. We must notice what the Universe is giving us and ask why.

After her experience, Fanny wrote a series of books to help women cope with life after a breast cancer diagnosis. The booklets are called *I Wish I Knew*. They have been published and distributed in multiple languages, helping thousands of women along the way. Fanny also made some dramatic life changes when she quit her stressful engineering job and moved from Boston to Tulum Mexico where she opened a yoga studio called Tribal Tulum. She currently runs the studio and leads personal yoga retreats, helping people heal through yoga. If you would like to learn more about her books or her studio and yoga retreats, visit thatbarrygirl.com and tribaltulum.com.

Financial loss is another life experience that can be devastating. I once heard an interview with singer-songwriter Leonard Cohen. He discovered after retiring that his business partner had embezzled most of his money and sold the rights to many of his songs. This situation forced him to return to touring and songwriting. He said this experience was a blessing in disguise. "Those were the most joyous years of my life."

Wayne Dyer, in his book *The Shift*, also shares some of his learning experiences.

> A heart attack helped me become more caring toward the suffering of others. Being in foster homes as a young boy taught me

self-reliance. A painful separation from my wife allowed me to write with a more compassionate heart. I now feel that any big challenge is an opportunity to grow.

I can fill an entire book with stories that support this Universal Truth. I simply want to emphasize that there is a light at the end of the tunnel if we can push through these challenging times and never stop looking for those seeds of wisdom. Again, it can take some time for these seeds to bloom. I guarantee you that when Fanny was being rolled into the operating room for her cancer surgery, she was not thinking, *What an amazing gift!*

Have patience. I promise this is not about God punishing you. We are being strengthened for a heroic mission that lies ahead. The Universe is a powerful teacher with good intentions. Since most people on the planet are stuck in this unconscious stage of life, we will continue to see a lot of pain, suffering, and dis-ease in our world.

Although I might be painting a bleak picture, this is a critical point in our journey. The Universe is leading us. This is how we grow and evolve. To understand what really happens, we must revisit our friends the Bodyguard and the Sleeping Giant. Up to this point, we have allowed our loyal Bodyguard to run the show. Remember, we created this "separate self" long ago as a means of survival on this alien planet. If you are reading this book right now, the Bodyguard has been successful. You are still alive!

Considering the crazy responsibilities we have given him, the Bodyguard has done a pretty good job. His primary role has been to protect and control the world around us. To make sure this fragile human being (me) is always happy, never gets his feelings hurt, and avoids all danger. Wow! What an awful job! Our Bodyguard is doing the best he can, considering this impossible task. This mind-made separate self has been giving us instructions for a very long time. This is why our "Monkey Mind" is so frazzled! As you might imagine, trying to *control the world* can be exhausting.

The School of Life, with its constant tests and trials, has worn the Bodyguard down. When he eventually grows weary, he will temporarily drop his guard. This is all part of the Game Plan. During this momentary rest, our mind is free to wander. With no outside control or influence, the mind will naturally wander within. Yes, this is a natural pull that we have never really felt before due to all the outside interference. In this time of weakness, we finally look within. Yahoo! Sound the trumpets! All the pain, suffering, and struggles of School were intended to lead us to this moment.

Why do we finally look within when given the opportunity? I believe we've simply become frustrated and are looking for different results. The Bodyguard had provided us many external solutions, trying to help us *fill*

the void. The School of Life has done its job! The pain has pushed us to redirect our focus. We have reached a point in our education that we demand more! This empty void must be filled, and these struggles must come to an end! When I say we finally "look within," I mean this literally. This is not some hocus-pocus concept. You will actually find yourself closing your eyes and saying to your Self, "I've had enough. What's next?"

During all this internal turbulence, the Sleeping Giant has grown restless and begins to awaken. Maybe he hears you call, "I've had enough. What's next?" If you were paying attention, you might have noticed during this self-talk that there is a speaker and a listener. The speaker is our physical self (BBM) using words or thoughts. The listener is our Divine Observer. If you missed this subtle interaction, it's not too late. You can try this simple exercise right now.

Find a quiet, private spot where you can sit for a moment. Close your eyes and say, "Hello, hello. Is anyone in there?" I know this sounds crazy, but give it a try. Don't forget to lock the door. It's best to say these words silently, in thought only. Don't look for a verbal response. If you hear one, this will only be your Bodyguard trying to interfere. I am simply asking you to recognize that your thoughts are being heard. Try it again. "Hello. Hello." Knowing there is a part of you that silently observes these thoughts is the first step to discovering your Divine Nature. Stay tuned. When we learn how to collaborate with this part of ourselves, your life will be transformed.

Discovery is a huge moment. I cannot emphasize enough how important it is to reach this level of the Game. Without Discovery, you cannot evolve and experience the joys of being a conscious player. The silence created by the temporary absence of the Bodyguard's relentless chatter allows you to reach this stage. The Sleeping Giant is now awake. The veil is briefly lifted, and you can feel the comfort of not being alone. When you reunite with your Divine Nature, that empty void is filled. You briefly experience a sense of oneness. Although this reunion will prove to be short-lived for now, this Discovery changes everything! This new awareness has activated a consciousness in every cell of your body. Life will never be the same.

This might be a good place for a quick timeout to discuss some spiritual terminology. I promised you a simple story that would demystify the spiritual path. I do not want any confusion over semantics. Since many of these terms are subject to debate, I will simply tell you how I define them. After all, words are just symbols for ideas. This explanation might help you better understand my ideas.

So, what did we just discover anyway? Is it the Soul? Is the Soul the same as God? Yes, in this stage of our evolution, we are discovering the Sleeping Giant, a.k.a. the Soul. I will occasionally substitute the term Higher Self for Soul. I believe we are all born into this world as Body and Soul. This Sleeping Giant lies dormant within all of us, waiting to be discovered. I see the Soul as Spirit manifest in man, an individualized reflection of God. In other words, if God were the ocean, the Soul would represent a drop of water from this ocean. This life-force is what connects us to each other and to all creation.

I see the Soul as the eternal part of my being, my connection to the Creator. I will often use the words Creator, Source, Divine, Universe, or Spirit interchangeably with God. I believe as human beings we all consist of Body, Soul and Spirit. As you will soon discover, the lines become blurred after Surrender. Actually, these lines are merely illusions of separation which will disappear entirely as we merge into one. Life becomes very simple after Surrender. No debate over spiritual terminology will be necessary after our reunion.

Okay, back to School. When the School of Life finally leads you to look within, you discover your Soul. This is your connection to the Divine. That's why it feels so freaking good! Even when we were unconscious sleepwalkers, we were never really separate from our Source. God patiently waited for you to make this discovery.

As explained earlier, the Game Plan was for the Soul to go into hibernation while the BBM went to School. We needed to learn the ropes and be strengthened for the awesome adventure that lies ahead. Hopefully you don't run out of time. *Free will* determines how long we linger at each stage. Most people do not make this Discovery until it's too late. According to those who have had near death experiences (NDEs), on your deathbed, all will be revealed. I once heard Anita Moorjani speak at a Hay House conference. She described her illness, coma, and NDE. Anita said, "After this experience I just wanted to grab people and shake them. Wake up! You are an amazing gift from God. Don't waste another moment!" Anita goes into great detail about her NDE in her amazing book *Dying to be Me.*

Although we finally get to graduate from School, this does not mean our spiritual journey has come to an end. When I first made this discovery, I thought I had arrived. *Hallelujah! My journey is now complete. I am an enlightened man.* Wow! Was I wrong. While I was getting all New-Agey, rediscovering my Divine Nature, I'd forgotten about my fearless Bodyguard, the loyal one who has been working 24/7 to protect me.

During the Bodyguard's brief rest, the mind is allowed to wander into this unknown realm. As a result, unsettled emotions bubble to the surface. Instinctively feeling a threat, the Bodyguard valiantly jumps back into action to "rescue" us from the unknown. Remember, the Bodyguard has gotten very good at his job. With renewed strength, he returns to his position, unaware of our temporary reunion with the Giant. We are now torn between our loyalty to the Bodyguard and our newfound connection to the Giant. The Bodyguard and the Giant will fight for our attention. An Epic Battle lies ahead.

SUMMARY

We must learn from the highs and lows of the human experience. We will get thru School quickly if we pay attention and look for the wisdom in all lessons. At some point on our journey, we are inspired to look within for guidance. The School of Life has done its job. All experiences in life have been designed to lead us to this moment. Although amnesia is a necessary part of our journey, so is remembering. Forgetting is *not* the root of all evil, but not remembering is a problem. We have somehow grown complacent in our discomfort and this Discovery was long overdue. This sets the stage for an Epic Battle. Do we remain complacent, following instructions from our loyal Bodyguard, or do we take the leap of faith and allow the Giant to lead the way?

Congratulations! You have made the most important Discovery of all time! You are now a seeker on your spiritual path. You are a conscious player in the Game of Life. Will you now find the courage to Surrender?

CHAPTER 3

THE EPIC BATTLE

After Discovery, life will never be the same. This is a good thing. The Giant is awake, and we now feel the pull of our Divine Nature. We still have hurdles to overcome. The Bodyguard is not ready to give up control of his kingdom. The Giant soon discovers he now has a roommate. To make matters worse, this roommate is a real control freak! Although this is a necessary part of the Game, the Giant is ready to return to his rightful throne. His first instinct is to force the Body Guard out! The two sides prepare for battle. This will be God's final testing ground. The School of Life was elementary compared to the Epic Battle. Some of our most difficult lessons will be presented during this stage.

Since we are now conscious, we can make choices that will directly affect the quality of our lives. With this new awareness comes responsibility. We are playing at a different level now. This drama will challenge the Body and Soul to evolve. Will the two sides learn enough during this lifetime to connect, or does the Soul return home empty-handed to await its next assignment? You see, the Soul has been through this process many times. The Body, a temporary vessel for the Soul, only gets one shot to figure this out. Will we learn to trust, allowing ourselves to be vulnerable enough to take that leap of faith? The outcome of this Epic Battle will determine your success in the Game of Life. Time is short. Be courageous. Do not waste this opportunity.

Truth be told, most of us will not reach the stage of Surrender. Although this Battle is a necessary part of our spiritual evolution, our *free will* determines how long we remain in this phase. Most of us will remain stuck way too long. This was me! I was lost in the Epic Battle for decades. I was happy and excited about my life-changing Discovery, but I was not ready to shake things up. I was scared. I enjoyed the feeling of this new connection, but I was spiritually naive and didn't know what to do with it. I had many unanswered questions.

- Why do I have to choose sides?
- No one ever taught me about Surrender. Does Surrender mean I need to give up all my stuff?
- Sure, this journey can be painful at times, but I can handle it. I have spent decades perfecting my persona (mask). Do I really want to give up now?

I had grown very comfortable being led by my trustworthy Bodyguard. I was simply not ready to step into the unknown.

After the initial rush of excitement associated with Discovery, the euphoria will soon be replaced by confusion. One of the biggest challenges will be accepting the Universal Law that says *God has always been with us. We have never been separated from God.* Although Discovery may feel like we have a new visitor, Spirit has always been with us, patiently waiting. The mere thought of this can instill feelings of panic, anger, or shame related to our many life experiences. If we live long enough, most of us will suffer through some terrible stuff. Before we accept this Universal Law, we will naturally ask, "Where were You? Why didn't You help me? How could You let this happen? Is this really true?" I have spent countless hours meditating on these questions. The answer that kept returning was "Yes! Not only was I with you during all of your experiences, but I allowed these things to happen." Ouch! Damn those Universal Laws! It took some serious Soul-searching before I was able to understand and accept this answer.

The most difficult life lessons are forgiveness, compassion, and unconditional love. These advanced lessons could not be taught in the School of Life. Strength and self-awareness are necessary. To truly embody these qualities, we need to go to some dark places. If being a victim isn't bad enough, at times we might actually need to experience playing the role of the bad guy. For example, let's say your mother was a bipolar alcoholic who would abuse you (emotionally and/or physically) when she was having a bad day. Fast forward ten years and you are now a young mother who occasionally lashes out at your child in fits of anger. Or maybe you were bullied as a child in school and discover that you have become a bully in your workplace as an adult. If you are aware enough to awaken during this process, you can learn the lesson and break the cycle.

You've gone to a dark place as a victim, and at times as the victimizer. As angry and ashamed as we feel, these experiences are often necessary to teach empathy, forgiveness, and compassion. The cycle of violence and abuse can be broken. All of God's creations deserve a path to healing, but we can't take our pain, hate, or anger with us. When you are ready to accept this Universal Law, you must forgive and love yourself before you can be available to help others.

If we are open enough to embrace this awareness, we can move through this process quickly. I am optimistic. A spiritual revolution is upon us! We must awaken now, or risk being left behind. We are moving into an enlightened age. Parents are teaching their children these Universal Laws and spiritual principles. When this happens, the vicious cycle of pain and suffering will come to an end. We have all paid a price for this wisdom. I've often said this awareness is a gift, but I am reconsidering this statement. This awareness is really a reward. You have earned it! Don't waste these painful experiences. The Epic Battle will leave scars. These scars are beautiful reminders of where we have been on this adventure. When we have the courage to Surrender, an amazing magical life awaits.

What steps can we take to get through this Battle as quickly as possible? You are now aware of the Divine within, and you will feel the constant pull of your inner guide. The Bodyguard will keep you busy with his relentless chatter, knowing you cannot hear the Giant through the noise. In a nutshell, this is the definition of our Epic Battle. The Bodyguard and the Giant are fighting for our attention. Being conscious, you now have the power to choose.

The choices we make during this phase of our journey will determine if we get to advance in this lifetime. To progress from Discovery to Surrender, we must accept these Universal Laws:

- Everything happens for a reason. No mistakes!
- If you ignore a life lesson, the Universe will try again. These experiences will gradually become more painful.
- God has been with you every step of the way.
- You were born into this world as Body and Soul, both equally important for this heroic mission.

One of the toughest questions you will need to ask yourself is this: am I going to allow some of the worst experiences of my past dictate my future? Why do we cling to these horrible experiences and feelings? I can understand wanting to hold on to some happy, blissful moment from the past, but what the hell am I doing clinging to the bad stuff? Holding on to anger, hate, or shame has no benefit! You are only poisoning yourself. With this understanding, I was ready to let go. I will admit this took some blind faith. I did not fully understand why bad things happen to good people. What I did know was that my life was a constant struggle, and I was exhausted. The Battle wore me down. Remember these words: "The Battle wore me down." It's time to sound the trumpets again!

This is another one of those huge moments. I just answered my own question. This is why bad things can happen to good people. This is all part of the Game. These "bad" experiences did exactly what they were designed to do. Once again, the Universe wore me down, forcing me to look within. These painful experiences actually rescue us from being stuck. No mistakes! Again, the more stubborn we are, the harder the lessons will become. A big decision is now at your doorstep. Do you continue following instructions from your loyal Bodyguard or is it time for a change? The Divine within patiently awaits your decision. Up until this moment, all events have been perfect and for your benefit, guiding you toward Surrender.

If you are still anxious about letting go, I will tell you what's on the other side. The drama, pain, and struggle associated with your everyday life will soon come to an end. You will begin to see past experiences in a new light. You begin to take back your power. You have made it through this Epic Battle and have the scars to prove it. You deserve a trophy! Don't be ashamed. Our scars should be considered sacred. Be proud of all the challenges you have overcome.

Why do we resist Surrender? Since I was one of the stubborn ones, spending decades lost in this Battle, I've spent a lot of time contemplating this question. Maybe you can relate to some of my excuses:

- **Fear of change**. The unknown can be scary. *My life might be a struggle now, but it feels predictable and safe. I've learned how to manage the painful moments. It's not all that bad.*

- **It's easier to be a victim**. Moving from being a victim to a conscious "player" in the Game of Life is very powerful. To admit you have this power means you must take responsibility for your current life conditions. Your external world is a direct reflection of your inner world. We must have the courage to accept this responsibility and do the work required for change. Most of us are not willing to do the work.

- **We feel shame for forgetting our Divine Nature**. We don't understand that "forgetting" is a natural part of our evolution process. Most of us have been brought up on traditional religious dogma to be God-fearing people worried about upsetting an external judgmental God. *OMG! I have been ignoring You for so long. I am sure it is too late for me.* At this stage, most of us are still unaware of the nurturing, loving, nonjudgmental God who resides within each of us.

- **What will others think of me?** *I don't want to appear weak. I have spent decades creating* *this facade.* This was the protective mask my Bodyguard helped me create.

- **I didn't really see an alternate group to join**. I considered "spiritual" people to be kind of weird. They didn't look like me, they dressed funny, and they used the G-word too much. No offense to the bearded turban-wearing teachers who still inspire me today. I know this sounds superficial, but at this stage on my path, I was not very courageous. Although I felt drawn to New Age teachings, I didn't have the courage to be open about it. I would secretly study these spiritual books and hide them from friends and family.

- **The Bodyguard and the Giant were simply not ready**. These two powerful forces viewed each other as enemies. In the early stages of this Battle, they were in no mood for Surrender, both considering themselves as rightful master of the kingdom! Until these two evolve, the Battle will continue.

- **I still felt a strong loyalty to my Bodyguard**. Although I was now aware of my Divine Nature, I created the Bodyguard long ago when I needed help. *I can't abandon him now!* We have all been misled by the so-called experts. Most of the self-help gurus talk about the need to kill the separate self. Yes, we are taught that to live happy lives we must eliminate the ego, personality, and everything associated with this "false self." What a bunch of crap! The Bodyguard and the Monkey always get a bad rap. The Bodyguard is a control freak, and the mind is a "monkey" because we assigned them an impossible task long ago: *"Control my world and protect me 24/7."* Talk about mission impossible!

- **Addictions keep the mind focused on the body**. Many of the external solutions we have tried to help "fill the void" have proven to be very addictive. Look around. We are all hooked on something (food, sugar, alcohol, drugs, sex, internet, porn, video games, etc.). These addictions distract us. Our human consciousness is forced to focus on feeding the monster. This makes it very difficult to have an authentic connection with Spirit.

Drug and alcohol abuse kept me feeling sick and tired for decades. I consider the *Alcohol Trap* to be a big reason why many of us struggle on this spiritual path. If you find yourself stuck in this trap, you are not alone. Over 70% of the adult population is with you. This elaborate trap, one that causes sickness, addiction, and death has been passed down from generation to generation. You never really had a chance. Everyone was in on this grand scheme. Ever since you were a child, the huge corporations have been grooming you to purchase their products. Do you really think strawberry kiwi wine coolers are made for adults? The state and federal governments generate billions of dollars from alcohol tax revenue. Our healthcare industry makes huge profits treating us from all our alcohol-related illnesses (diseases of the stomach, liver, pancreas, cancers, dementia, depression, etc.). Finally, consider our friends and family who can't wait until we are old enough to join their "fun." Most have good intentions, blind to the trap they are in. Others are aware, but fear being alone. Have you heard the old saying "Misery loves company"? You can download the complete article "The Alcohol Trap" from my website. I share some of my thoughts on this global epidemic, which is responsible for delaying our spiritual growth.

Knowledge is power and climbing out of this trap is challenging but achievable. If I can do it, anyone can! Like a magician revealing the secrets of a trick, with this new insight, you can never be fooled again. In Annie Grace's book *This Naked Mind*, many of the myths related to this elaborate trap are exposed. For me, the path to freedom was understanding how the mind was tricked and having faith in the Universal Law that says *everything happens for a reason*. One of my favorite quotes from Annie's book can be found on page 206:

> And now you have the advantage. You've experience alcohol addiction and now you know how vile and insidious it is. I have a perspective that the non-drinker doesn't have. I've seen the evils first hand. Survival deserves a medal, not a stigma. I am stronger than before. I now have a shield of experiential armor. I feel strong enough to stand up and fight.

Again, what doesn't kill you makes you stronger. Don't be anonymous! Wear your scars like a badge of courage to inspire others. We can use this wisdom for many of life's challenges. I have experienced [fill in the blank], and now I have the advantage! Surrender was my path to freedom. Once my new programmer was back in charge, my addictions naturally melted away.

If you haven't figured it out yet, the Epic Battle is a very challenging stage. As I've said, this is God's final testing ground. Until we learn to be appreciative of our Bodyguard and love our Monkey, Surrender will not be possible.

The Bodyguard has gotten very good at his job and has no plans to be forced out. If you chose to follow the experts' advice, you will be stuck in this battle for a very long time. Don't feel bad. You are not alone. Go to any bookstore and you will find volumes of self-help books explaining how to live a happy life, based on this faulty notion of killing the separate self and silencing the Monkey. Good luck with that!

I am here to tell you that there is a better way. Actually, I have learned it's the *only* way. The good news is that no part of you needs to be killed! I am trying to lead you on a path to merger, not murder. These facets of our Human Nature have played a very important role in our lives, and with a little guidance, they will continue to serve us on the mission that lies ahead. This is a huge deal! If you can grasp this concept, the Battle will come to an end. You will discover that the spiritual path is easy and enjoyable when we learn to embrace our separate self. This is a major step in our evolution. All we need to do is expand our awareness a little and allow ourselves to turn within and trust.

When you understand that you were born into this world as Body and Soul, *both equally important*, you will be on your way to freedom. Think about this. When the Bodyguard trusts that the Giant is not out to kill him, he will stop fighting so hard. He will begin to listen. This survival instinct is part of our Human Nature. When we feel threatened, we push back. Like any relationship, when we sincerely convey the other person's importance, the bond will strengthen and grow. Again, it takes two to tango. Responsibility for getting over this trust-hurdle is not all on the Bodyguard. Can the Giant change his forceful ways and learn to become a peacemaker?

This reminds me of a popular Bible quote, "The meek shall inherit the earth." This quote is often misunderstood.

Something was lost in translation. The word *meek* is misleading, given its modern-day interpretation as being submissive. The original Greek word written in ancient texts was *praotes*. The actual translation is "gentle strength, to display the right blend of force with a spirit of caring." With the proper translation, I was able to relate more to this teaching and how it effects our evolution on this adventure. When Body and Soul can demonstrate *praotes*, we shall inherit the earth.

Hopefully, through our experiences on the battlefield, we will soon come to understand this truth. When the Giant learns to soften, the Bodyguard will have the courage to surrender the illusion of control and need for protection. A shift begins to occur. The ultimate goal during this stage is to Surrender control to the Soul. This is your primal way. You can only fight against Mother Nature for so long. Like a raging river, the natural flow will eventually prevail. The river will wear down all obstacles. If you need some proof of this, visit the Grand Canyon.

As human beings, we don't have millions of years to wait for this process to unfold. If we want to be fulfilled in this lifetime, we need to act now. How can we help the Soul regain control of the throne? We've already learned, the Bodyguard is too strong and stubborn to be forced out. What if the Giant becomes a peacemaker? Maybe as a peaceful warrior, the Soul can persuade the Bodyguard of his importance. History has shown that all successful mergers have required master negotiators. A foundation of trust and faith must be established to create a true partnership. The use of force only produces temporary results. Can the Bodyguard be convinced that he will not be killed? Can he be assured that he will be an important player after the merger? Yes! Not only is this possible, but it is the only way to win at this Game.

Considering the Bodyguard is just a facet of the human mind, maybe we can learn to use logic as a path to Surrender? Let's explore this approach. I am hoping at this point in our adventure, we all have a basic understanding of the Law of *No Mistakes*. I believe all of God's expressions are very intentional. With this understanding, consider these logical questions:

- Why would God go through the trouble of creating this amazing human being, each with its own unique essence (personality, character, skills), only to kill this amazing creation upon Surrender? This would be like saying God made a mistake. Using logic, the simple fact that we exist should help persuade the Bodyguard of his importance!

- If the purpose of creation is for God to express on earth, how the heck is He supposed to do this without us? How many burning bushes can there be? Maybe the messengers can be ghostlike characters descending from the heavens. How would humankind handle this? I'm guessing we would figure out a way to kill these messengers too. Yes, God needs you for this adventure! This includes your body, personality, character, and even the infamous ego.

- Why would so much effort be put into our training if we are going to be eliminated upon awakening? The Universe has spent many years training and strengthening us for our heroic mission.

If the human brain can understand this argument, maybe the Giant will have a chance, but time is running out. He will use every tool possible to convince the Bodyguard of his importance, including logic.

> *There are no mistakes. Kill you? No freaking way! You are an important piece of the puzzle. We cannot finish the Game without you. God expresses through us! This is not a trick. I need you exactly where you are.*

In the Bhagavad Gita, Arjuna argues that it would be sinful to slay our enemies. The high scriptures teach us to live in harmony. Arjuna goes on to say, "These sensory instruments were divinely created for man to exist in the Universe." Krishna then explains,

> We are not to destroy these sense instruments. The devotee is not being asked to blind his eyes or deafen his ears, but to slay their bad habits which keep the Soul imprisoned.

As I argue throughout this book, we don't need to kill the ego: we just need to tame it! This is similar to breaking a wild horse. The master is not trying to kill this magnificent creature. We are attempting to reach an agreement or a compromise. If successful, a powerful partnership will be formed.

Every "Body" that finds himself trapped in the Bodyguard's protective bubble will eventually feel imprisoned. When the Bodyguard has the courage to lay down his sword, we will all live in blissful harmony as one. Paramahansa Yogananda refers to this expression of self as "the purified ego." He also says,

> The sensory functions have their rightful place in man's life only after he has subordinated them by realizing himself as the Soul, one with Spirit. Not a body dominated by the

senses. We must be securely anchored in our
true Divine Nature.

Don't be skeptical of this message because you feel
your position in life is menial. Upon awakening, you
will find yourself exactly where you are needed most. You
might be a housewife, a construction worker, a doctor, a
CEO or a carpenter. As Shakespeare wrote,

> All the world is a stage and all the men and
> women are merely players. They have their
> exits and their entrances and one man in his
> time *plays* many parts.

The key word in this quote is *play*. We need to
Surrender and become conscious players in this
amazing Game. It is time to *play your part*. You are on
a covert mission, embedded amongst the sleepwalkers.
Will Body and Soul find the gentle strength needed to
surrender their weapons and merge? This reunion is
necessary for God to express on earth. Everyone asks the
same questions. "Why are we here? What is the purpose
of life? What is the purpose of creation?" Well, this is it!
We were born into this world as one (Body/Soul/Spirit).
Our Divine Nature took the backseat, while we learned
the ropes and became street-smart. It is now time to
reunite for our heroic mission.

As a child of God, this is your birthright. You were born into royalty! Although Spirit will patiently wait to be discovered, time is short. These bodies only last so long. You have the power to end this Battle now. Don't let your time expire without experiencing the Game played at its highest level.

For me, Surrender was not a lightning bolt moment of inspiration, although I believe it can be for some. This was more of a gradual awakening. I also got lucky and stumbled upon some magic words. *Is there more to life than this?* Like Ali Baba saying, *"Open sesame,"* this too opened a door to hidden treasures. Don't get me wrong. I definitely got hit over the head with the club a lot. Eventually I began to accept the Universal Laws. History has proven these truths time and time again. I have personally lived through enough "bad" experiences that turned out to be blessings in disguise. I slowly began to look at the world differently. It started to become clear that the Universe was working for me, not against. All experiences became learning opportunities. This awareness represents the beginning of the end to this Battle.

This is a blissful place. The pain and suffering related to the constant lessons, tests, and trials will soon come to an end. Life begins to flow naturally. Unfortunately, we delay Surrender because we have gotten comfortable with the pain and suffering in life. We believe life is supposed to be a struggle. We think we can have it both ways. We want to hang on to our "normal life" and occasionally check in with our spiritual side. *I go to church on Sundays. I'm good.* Being aware is not enough. We have decisions to make. Many of us have reached the Discovery stage, aware of a Soul essence within, but we were not ready to commit. If you are lucky, you will get the call several times throughout your life. Do you now have the courage to answer?

Spoiler alert! There are higher levels waiting for us beyond Discovery. In the end, many people will say, "I didn't know." You can no longer use this excuse. You can't put the genie back in the bottle. When you understand this process, Surrender will become easy because it is our natural state of being. I am not asking you *to do* something. I am asking you to *stop doing* something. Think about this concept. Shouldn't it be easy to stop fighting?

On the rare occasion your mind is quiet, you will feel the pull from within. You will see your True Self. Unfortunately for many, we quickly look away. The mere thought of Surrender scares the hell out of us. If this is you, I have great news! You don't need to give up your life when you Surrender. A lot of time and energy has been invested into your persona (mask) and your place in the world. You get to be an undercover agent on a heroic mission. How much fun is that? The need to give up your life or your "stuff" is just another misconception about the spiritual path. This is exactly the kind of bullshit the Bodyguard wants us to believe to support his fight to retain the throne. Material and sensory pleasures are not evil. Even the Gita teaches,

> Evil lies only in the misuse of the products
> and power of nature. Enjoyment of this
> abundance when free from attachment will
> be expressed in noble achievements.

I believe the riches of the world were intended to be enjoyed by all. This idea was reinforced by Wayne Dyer at a Hay House conference I attended in New York. Someone in the audience questioned Wayne's wealth and how it related to his spirituality. Wayne was unapologetic in his response. "Yes, I have a beautiful home in Maui. I also have homes in California and Florida. The Universe wants us all to be abundant." I love it!

When the veil is temporarily lifted, and we begin to understand the illusionary nature of the physical world, *attachment* becomes a pointless idea. I would like to take this thought one step further. What if our awareness could make the veil transparent or lucid? What if we could live a lucid life? I am sure everyone has experienced vivid dreams while sleeping. When the alarm awakens you in the morning, it's almost embarrassing how real the dream felt! You might be sweating because someone was chasing you or crying because your feelings were hurt. You will have this same type of awakening when your Soul leaves the Body at the time of your death. Similar to your alarm going off in the morning, you will quickly discover this life was also a vivid dream. Like in your sleeping dream, everything that seemed so real will vanish in an instant. In this moment, we will realize how much energy was wasted worrying about all of our material possessions. The good news is that we don't have to wait for death to benefit from this awareness. We can begin living a *lucid life* today!

To better understand this concept of lucidity, let's take a moment to explore our lucid dreams. You are asleep at night having a dream but not completely absorbed by the dream state. In other words, you are aware that you are having a dream. This lucid state is fun! Knowing you are in a dream world gives you the freedom to be fearless. We can enjoy the experience because we are aware of the illusion. Similar to this lucid dream, we can enjoy lucid living now. When we live a lucid life, aware of the illusion, we can enjoy this temporary adventure without fear or attachment. Lucidity gives us the freedom to live big and bold. Don't let your alarm go off only to discover you never had the courage to express your True Self. Sorry, no snooze button on this alarm.

Most humans today are either unconscious students in the School of Life, or seekers, aware of their Divine Nature, but still engaged in the Epic Battle. If we find ourselves in one of these stages, we obviously have more to learn. Although you can't skip any steps, *free will* does determine how much time you will spend at each level. The seeker is aware and has a choice to make. *Will I continue to follow the instructions from my Bodyguard, or am I ready to Surrender control to the Giant?*

This might be a good time to discuss the word *surrender*. For most of us, this word carries a negative connotation. If you look up surrender in the dictionary, you will find the following: "to give up, cease resistance to the enemy, to lose." Am I really telling you the ultimate goal in the Game of Life is to surrender? That sounds like a bunch of crap! This is funny, since the Surrender I am referring to will be a joyful, blissful experience. When we gain the strength and wisdom needed to reconnect with our Divine Nature, we will emerge as powerful beings. This Surrender is a choice. This will never be forced on you. You must reach a point where you don't give a shit what anyone else thinks! Although this might sound selfish, it's imperative. Before we can become supernatural and be of service to the world, we must be true to ourselves.

As Brené Brown says, "We must have the courage to stand alone in the wilderness." When Maya Angelou speaks about being authentic, she says, "The price is high, but the rewards are great." We need to stop using the opinions of others as an excuse. Drop your guard and have the courage to be vulnerable for just a moment. The veil will be lifted. You will clearly see your true nature, and the illusion of being separate will vanish in an instant. When this occurs, a powerful force becomes activated in your life. The rewards of Surrender will be instant. The results you see in your life will be all the proof you need. You reunite as one, which is how you were born into this world. This is your natural state of being.

The *big* question is this: will these two sides work out their differences before it's too late? Will the Bodyguard have the courage to stop resisting, or does the Soul return to its Source empty-handed again? Will Body and Soul successfully reach the highest levels of this Game by evolving and merging to become true players during this awesome adventure? When we Surrender, we are transformed. The three become one (Body-Soul-Spirit). When I was searching for a word to describe this transformation, I looked up *supernatural* in the dictionary. The definition was perfect: "a creative force beyond the laws of nature: God-like." From now on, I will refer to the state of Surrender as becoming a <u>super</u>natural hu<u>man</u>, which is our ultimate goal on this journey. Let's go with Super-Man for short (man is an abbreviation for human: no reference to gender). This is when the magic begins.

How do I become Super-Man? This is one of the many rewards of Surrender. This is where our *free will* comes into play. This process can be long or short. My Bodyguard was very stubborn. He always felt threatened when I started to communicate with the Giant. If you set aside time for daily meditation, an inner dialogue will begin. The Bodyguard gradually begins to soften. He begins to relinquish control, allowing the Giant to guide us. With this Soul guidance, life begins to flow effortlessly. The Bodyguard will begin to see the Giant as a powerful friend. The Universe will reward us when we begin to take direction from the Soul. The Bodyguard can't argue with the results. He begins to trust and allow suggestions from the Giant to direct our thoughts and actions. In other words, we are finally allowed to follow our inner guide. For a short time, we experience being *in the zone*. This is actually our Primal Way, our Divine Nature at work! We would always be *in the zone* if we could only learn to Surrender.

Although the Bodyguard still feels vulnerable, he continues to allow the Giant's input. His fear and need to control begin to fade. This is a bittersweet time. He understands that his original role in this life will soon become obsolete. It eventually becomes obvious that the Body would be best served by surrendering control to the Giant. At last, the Bodyguard takes the leap and Surrenders. The Battle has come to an end. With open arms and a weary smile, the two embrace.

This would be a good time for fireworks! Decades of tests and trials have led to this moment. All experiences during this challenging stage of life were designed to lead us to this moment.

After taking this leap of faith, the loyal Bodyguard anxiously awaits his fate. Much was promised during the Battle. When the dust settles, the reward of Surrender is revealed. The Bodyguard learns of his promotion. The meager man-made job of *guarding the body* has been elevated to Guardian Angel. This is perfect! Who better to fill this role? No one knows me better. This is truly a win-win situation. My loyal friend will continue to be by my side. Instead of trying to shield me from the world, my Guardian Angel will now assure that my path in the world is made clear for the heroic mission that lies ahead.

By revealing how the Battle ends, you can now be fearless! Many others have gone before you. The veil has been lifted, and you can hear the calling from within. *I need your help to carry out My mission. You are My channel for expression on this earth. You have infiltrated the unconscious world of the sleepwalkers. I need you!* Being an undercover agent on a covert mission is an exciting place to be. Are you ready?

We have reached a critical junction. For those of you who feel a connection to what I am saying, please continue with me on this adventure. In the following pages, I will attempt to explain how to Surrender in practical terms. Now that your human consciousness is ready and willing, the rest will be easy. You will get the full support of the Universe.

For those who are not yet ready to let go, I understand. I was in your shoes for decades. If you insist on being pissed off at the world, clinging to the past with guilt, regret, and anger, this is your choice. You can stay in this Battle as long as needed. The Bodyguard will continue to shield you from life. Fortunately, the Epic Battle will eventually lead us all to Surrender. The day will come when we realize our protective bubble has become a prison. Celebrate when this day arrives. It will be time to move from surviving to thriving.

Summary

After Discovery, we become seekers. Although we primarily associate with our Human Nature (BBM), we are now aware. We feel the pull of the Divine within and are always *seeking* opportunities to reconnect. It often feels like a tug-of-war between the Bodyguard and the Giant. This sets the stage for the Epic Battle. Many spiritual teachers talk about the need to kill the Bodyguard, which includes our personality, intellect, and ego. We are led to believe this separate self is evil. Not only is this wrong, but it's the single biggest reason most of humanity will remain stuck in this drama for ages. All facets of our Human Nature are perfect. We were born into this world as Body and Soul, both equally important. There are no mistakes. God needs us both to express on earth. We will all eventually become aware of this Universal Law. If you are one of the lucky few who makes it through the Epic Battle in this lifetime, you will find yourself stronger and wiser than when you first began this journey. Surrender is near.

CHAPTER 4

SURRENDER

Congratulations! If you are still reading this book, you have not only discovered your True Self, but you have also surrendered to your primal way. Your life is about to change dramatically! It's time to *dance with the one that brought you.*

This ancient Indian fable perfectly describes the process of surrendering to our primal way:

> Once upon a time, a lioness fell asleep with her baby cub in the jungle. As the mother slept, the cub wandered off into the darkness and was lost. Days later, on the verge of starvation, the cub was found by a flock of sheep. The sheep welcomed the cub and raised him as their own. Over time, the cub lost all awareness of his true self. The adolescent lion now acted, sounded, and behaved like a sheep.
>
> One hot day while grazing in a field, the sheep were startled by a large beast emerging from the forest. In a panic, they quickly ran in the opposite direction. The lion-sheep was frozen with fear. With great confusion, the beast approached and let out a roar that shook the earth! Assuming the end was near, the lion-sheep was paralyzed. The magnificent lion grabbed the trembling animal and asked, "Why do you live and act like a sheep when you are king of the jungle?" The lion-sheep did not respond. The

powerful lion pulled the sheepish lion to the water's edge. Forcing the cowardly lion's head toward his reflection, the frustrated beast exclaimed, "Look! We are the same! Let me hear you roar." In an effort to appease the beast, the lion let out sheep-like whimper. "Again!" demanded the beast. After several attempts, the lion began to hear a familiar roar. With this discovery, the timid lion began to feel a stirring within his body. Memories of his True Self were awakening.

The young lion stood on the river's edge, feeling a new sense of purpose and excitement. With this excitement came fear of the unknown. This discovery changed his world in an instant. The large beast began to walk back to the forest, turning to let out one final roar as if to say, "Are you coming?"

The young lion quickly realized his day of reckoning had arrived. Does he continue living his safe, predictable life as a sheep or does he embrace his True Self and surrender to the world of the unknown?

Looking at the beautiful forest on the horizon, the young lion decides to take the leap of faith. This lion chose to surrender, to return to his primal way, to become who he has always been: King of the Jungle.

It is time to stop behaving like sheep! As in this fable, Surrender is simply allowing your True Self to regain control. In the beginning of the book, I said that *man cannot serve two masters.* At that time, it was necessary for the Bodyguard to take control. We had no choice and welcomed this protection. At a very young age, we were still aware of both worlds. We were aware of the mask, protecting our vulnerable Soul. We have now gone full circle. We have awakened and are once again aware of our mask. We are now operating from a place of strength, not from the fear we experienced in early development. The Bodyguard has done his job, and it's time to pass the torch. Once again, man cannot serve two masters. You now have the power to choose, and you have chosen the Giant to lead. You have evolved. The Soul has regained control of his throne.

I love Carl Jung's quote about this process of evolution from his book *The Stages of Life.*

Thoroughly unprepared, we take the step into the afternoon of life. Worse still, we take this step with the false assumption that our truths and ideals will serve us as before. But we cannot live the afternoon of life according to the program of life's morning. What was true in the morning will at evening have become a lie.

Although you are a magnificent physical creation (Body, Brain, and Mind), like any supercomputer, we are only as good as the programmer inputting the instructions. Until now, we happily took instructions from the Bodyguard. However, it's time for an upgrade. The Giant is awake and restless. You feel the pull. You are now aware. We've all spent more time than we would like to admit trying to serve two masters during the Epic Battle. Surviving is not enough! The Bodyguard finally realized he was holding you back. With love and courage, he willingly surrendered to the Giant. The controls of this supercomputer (you) have been returned to the Master Programmer. We can now play at the highest level of the Game.

In this moment, everything changes. Stop! Please don't speed past this idea. This moment is everything. This is the purpose of creation. Body and Soul have evolved during this earthly drama and have reunited. Surrender is part two of man's primal purpose. You have now *filled the void*. We have all been unknowingly craving a return to our primal way. Going through the Epic Battle was our path from Discovery to Surrender. The Game does not end with Surrender. This is actually where the fun begins! Body and Soul will jump for joy. The illusion of separation has been dissolved, and the struggle to remain separate has come to an end. What a freaking relief!

Does this mean "bad" things will never happen to me again? Unfortunately, bad stuff will still happen in life. People will die, hearts will be broken, and accidents and illnesses are still possible. However, with this new awareness, how you see the world changes dramatically. Change your mind and what you see will change. When you surrender the illusion of control and need for protection, you will begin to see life as the amazing adventure it was intended to be.

The Universe will continue to unfold as it has been for 13.8 billion years, with or without your input. We have very little control. One of civilization's many problems is that we take ourselves too seriously, giving ourselves too much credit and too much blame. One of my favorite authors is Michael "Mickey" Singer who wrote *The Untethered Soul* and *The Surrender Experiment*. Mickey says, "We are nothing but a speck of dirt on a planet spinning in the middle of nowhere." The first time I heard Mickey say this, it made me laugh, but it also made me think. Such a simple truth, yet so powerful!

Consider everything that has happened over the past 13.8 billion years that has led to this moment in time. Planets and stars have burned brightly and have been extinguished. There have been violent collisions and explosions throughout the Universe. Entire species have come and gone on our planet. Now think of all the small things that have occurred just over the past couple hundred years that have led to *your* creation. For example, what if your great grandparents didn't meet after arriving from Europe? What if your father didn't miss his train, which led him to meeting your mother at the coffee shop by the train station? Everyone could probably agree that many events and chain reactions have occurred over the billions of years to bring us to this moment in time. When we open our eyes in the morning and look out at this amazing world that is still in the process of creation, what do we do? We look out and say, "I don't like it." Billions of years of creation are unfolding before our eyes, and we have the nerve to say, "I don't like it!" We have a wide variety of reasons or preferences to justify why we are unhappy.

- I don't like waking up this early.
- It's cold outside.
- It's hot outside.
- My kids are irritating.
- My boss is an ass.
- I hate my job.

OMG. We all need a serious shift in awareness! A true master opens his eyes in the morning, looks out at the world and thinks, *Wow, this is amazing!* A master is free to experience life as it naturally unfolds. He embraces it all with no preference. Mickey says, "Every moment of every day should be lived like it's an amazing surprise party. This is Surrender."

Unfortunately, over our lifetime, most of us have created a long list of preferences that make it nearly impossible to be happy! We might have some brief moments when we get lucky and all of our preferences align, but these are fleeting moments. When we surrender this illusion of control, what we see will begin to change immediately!

This is a matter of choice. Your life as a spiritual master can start today. Embrace the "surprise party life" Mickey Singer talks about. Why not? The world is going to unfold in front of you whether you like it or not, so why not embrace it all? This is spirituality. Yes, you get to choose to be happy or miserable. What you choose will not change what is happening on the outside, so why not choose to be happy and amazed all the time?

In hindsight, I don't know what the hell I was thinking. Life was unfolding, and I was pissed off! I was kicking, screaming, and fighting the whole way! "No, I don't like it!" I sounded like a child. This is why the School of Life is so painful for most of us. As sleepwalkers, we don't have this awareness. We don't know that we can choose how we react to the world. Although I have said *to strive for a life of meaning is much more significant than the endless pursuit of happiness*, when given a choice between misery and happiness, I will always choose to be happy.

I am blessed that my wife also lives by Mickey's *surprise party* principle. Again, bad stuff can still happen. Challenging events will still cross your path. When they do, my wife and I often look at each other and laugh. We now have this inside joke. We race to see who will be the first to shout, "Surprise!" This does not mean we are submissive or passive. To the contrary, when you are not attached to a specific outcome, you are coming from a place of strength. You are no longer paralyzed with anger, fear, or resentment when something goes "wrong." We now understand that life will unfold naturally, and the Universe is always working in our favor. In every adversity lie seeds of wisdom. I love the Jason Mraz song lyric, "You win some and you learn some" from the song *I'm Yours*. We take action and continue to learn from life's lessons. Sometimes we are laughing together, and sometimes we are crying, but we are no longer fighting with life. The struggle is over.

When I first became a seeker on my spiritual journey, I hired an amazing life coach named Elaine Christine. Elaine has been my dear friend and spiritual counselor for decades. She once told me,

> Spiritual masters are ready and willing to experience *all* feelings life has to offer. We will experience some incredible joyous

feelings mixed with some gut-wrenching pain and sorrow. It's all part of this adventure. It will all pass, if we let it.

I didn't understand this concept when Elaine first tried to explain, but in hindsight, it's so obvious. All feelings are beautiful. Think about the people who pay good money to sky dive, ride roller coasters, or go to haunted houses. Talk to them afterward, and they will probably say, "It was amazing. Made me feel so alive!" Have you ever heard someone explain a sad movie? "It was so good! I cried for two hours."

Unfortunately, in real life, at the first hint that something will be uncomfortable, we try to distract or numb ourselves. We try to push the feelings down. Many of us turn to drugs, alcohol, food, etc. to avoid *feeling*. These techniques might work temporarily, but in the end only delay our evolution. In order to Surrender, we must stop fighting against life. We must embrace it all. Feeling these emotions is part of our Human Nature. Both the ecstasy in joy and the pain of sorrow make you feel alive. You don't get to choose how life unfolds, but you do get to choose how you react. If you suppress your feelings, you are fighting against the natural flow of life and delaying the experience. If you can learn to embrace it all, you will be on your way to the freedom of Surrender.

Surrender is a purifying process. Memories that once haunted us are now free to be released. The Bodyguard is no longer in charge, suppressing these feelings in order to protect us. Since we did not allow the energy from our traumatic experiences to pass through us, we've created blockages. This trapped energy can be stuck in our bodies for a lifetime. These blockages interfere with our body's natural ability to heal. Scientific studies now show that ailments such as inflammation, nerve disorders, chronic pain, IBS, headaches, depression, and fatigue, can often be traced back to this emotional trauma from childhood. The good news is we now have the awareness to allow this blocked energy to pass.

Mickey Singer explains in his book *The Untethered Soul* that during the normal course of our daily lives, we will all have experiences that "bump into our thorns." Mickey explains these thorns as "trapped emotions in the body." We should be grateful for these disturbances and allow this energy to escape. As Mickey says, "Do not push these feelings back down!" This is an opportunity to clear this crap from our system. Lean back, take a deep breath, drop your shoulders, and let these emotions rise to the surface. You are now aware. Be the observer of the process. You're not a child anymore. You can handle some discomfort. Allow yourself to cry, scream, and do whatever. When it passes, you will be free. Please check out *The Untethered Soul* and *The Surrender Experiment*. Mickey goes into great detail about the process of removing your thorns.

Surrender is not some hocus-pocus concept that can only be experienced by a highly evolved spiritual master. Well, you do need to be evolved, but if you're reading this book, you are already a seeker on this excellent adventure. Give yourself some credit: you have evolved! You are no longer a sleepwalker. You have endured the School of Life and fought your way through the Epic Battle. You have earned this awareness! If you are ready to move from a philosophical idea of Surrender to the real-life practical expression, I would like to share some tips that have helped me.

In addition to our body's need for physical exercise, we also need to exercise our spiritual muscles. A daily practice of meditation, visualization, and affirmation is critical. To sharpen our communication skills with our Inner Guide, we must make a habit of quieting the busy mind. Meditation reduces the noise and distractions, making it easier to hear this guidance. Did you notice I did not say *we need to silence the monkey mind?* This is a ridiculous concept. Your mind is an amazing supercomputer working for you 24/7. Staying with this computer analogy, we might need to create a partition or firewall while we are meditating, but I don't want my Monkey to stop working! I just need a little quiet time.

When we assign a task to our Monkey, he will work tirelessly until finding a solution. Who wants to mess with that? I like to imagine sticking my head into the Monkey's office and saying, "Excuse me, I don't want to interrupt you, but I am going to close this door for a few minutes. I am grateful for all you do." It's a mind game, but it works for me.

Frequency and repetition help form any new habit. Every few hours, find a quiet spot and close your eyes for a couple of minutes. Set a recurring alarm on your phone if it helps. Don't say you can't. That's BS! Lock yourself in the bathroom if you must. Okay, now simply close your eyes and take a few slow deep breaths. Silently count to eight on the in-breath and eight on the out-breath. Focusing on breath and counting will redirect your attention. These minibreaks allow you to strengthen your connection with Source, your new Programmer. The way I see it, during our daily meditations, we are recharging our battery and the power source is Spirit. Similar to recharging your cell phone, we need to close all of our apps (eliminate distractions) and plug in.

After meditation, we can return to our daily activities at *full strength*. You will be astonished by the amount of energy that now flows through you. So much was wasted during the Battle. Anxiety, fear, and worry were draining your battery. Although the feeling of being *connected* during meditation can be amazing, we must return to our worldly duties. God created us for a reason. Our heroic mission awaits! Recharge and get busy!

Imagination is the engine for manifestation; therefore, practicing creative visualization is also extremely important. Like meditation, there have been many amazing books written on this subject. I am simply a student who has experienced the benefits. The simplified explanation I can offer you is this: When we create vivid pictures in our minds of our ideal life or our ideal world, we begin the process of manifesting. We are setting the stage for these events. The most important ingredients that still need to be added are the *emotions and feelings* associated with these wishes fulfilled.

Warning: Be careful what you wish for. Thoughts become things. Like it or not, we have been unconsciously manifesting our entire lives. Your outer world is a direct reflection of your past thoughts, feelings, and images. Imagination is the mind of God. When we reach the stage of Surrender, this Universal Mind becomes an extension of our human minds. We must learn to harness this power. I like to call this *creative consciousness*. We now have the power to collaborate with the Creator. In Dr. Joe Dispenza's book *Becoming Supernatural*, Dr. Joe goes into great detail explaining this proven formula of meditation combined with visualization. For the skeptics, he also includes real-life case studies with tons of scientific feedback to support the results.

The third exercise for strengthening those spiritual muscles would be the use of affirmations. Affirmations are a powerful tool. I like to think of them as code used for programming my supercomputer. After surrendering control to the Master Programmer, I want to make sure this channel of communication is wide open every day. I repeat my affirmations just before meditating. My favorite mantra is what I like to call the six magic words: *I devote my self to You*. I repeat this frequently throughout the day. These words are not only my abbreviated definition of Surrender, but they are also the foundation of my daily practice.

Do you remember the goofy exercise from the beginning of the book when I was trying to convince you that we are not alone *inside*? I asked you to close your eyes and say, "Hello, hello. Is anyone in there?" This exercise was designed to make you wonder, *Who is this "silent observer" of my human chatter?* When I am communicating with my Higher Self through these affirmations and meditations, I am communing with this Silent Observer. I don't need to do the "*hello, hello*" routine anymore. I know this is my Divine Nature that now guides me through life, on duty 24/7, always listening and waiting to comfort and guide me. How awesome is that?

We have the most powerful partner ever, just waiting for us to recognize Him and Surrender. This conscious communication is what makes us different from the world of sleepwalkers. The common man only gets to use his five senses. Super-Man has the sixth sense of intuition. You have discovered your power and it's time to learn how to use it. Every day going forward, this awareness will expand. Secrets will be revealed. As Super-Man, we will gradually develop this sixth sense.

When you begin your daily practice of collaborating with Spirit (affirmations, visualizations, and meditation), always remember to turn your focus within. Most of us were taught as children to look up into the sky when praying. We were taught to pray to an external, judgmental God who lives up in the clouds somewhere. For me, the imagery was of an old white man with a flowing beard. Maybe this works best for children. After all, explaining God as an energy or life-force that animates all of creation would be too much for most kids to grasp.

Did you know the Latin root for *animate* is *anima* and *animat,* which means "spirit, soul, to instill with life"? Anyway, since I am offering you practical steps to change your life post-Surrender, step #1 should be to *look inward when communicating with God.* You're not a child anymore. The Divine resides within. You are hosting God. This might seem like an insignificant detail, but it represents a very important shift. Inward focus is really a prerequisite for a successful meditation practice.

One of my favorite affirmations, which I recite several times per day, is the following:

> I am this body they call Craig.
> This is *Our* disguise.
> I am aware of my Divine Nature.
> I devote my self to You.
> We are One.

Since I have this memorized, I probably repeat it ten times per day. I close my eyes and take a fifteen-second timeout. This is very powerful for me. Every word in these five lines means a lot. Let me break it down.

1. *I am this body they call Craig.*

   I am first acknowledging my body, which is an important vehicle for God's expression. A gift from the Creator. At the same time, I am aware that I am much more than this physical form. When I say, "they call Craig," I'm playing with the idea of being aware of the "mask."

2. *This is Our disguise.*

   It's fun for me to think of being an undercover agent on a heroic mission. I strongly believe this spiritual path should be a fun adventure. You get to be 007 on a covert mission. The word

"Our" is capitalized because I know my Higher Self lies beneath the mask.

3. *I am aware of my Divine Nature.*
   I am simply acknowledging the Divine within. I am communicating with my Higher Self, the silent observer who is listening 24/7. It's kind of like saying, "*I see you.*"

4. *I devote my self to You.*
   These six magic words are huge. This statement reconfirms my commitment to Surrender. It is also a call to action, which I will discuss in the next chapter. There is significance between the lower case "self" and the capitalized "You." This small *self* is my human consciousness happily merging with the Divine within. Powerful stuff!

5. *We are One.*
   Although it was easy for me to *feel the oneness* after Surrender, it is very difficult to explain using words. It's almost like we don't have the language necessary. Therefore, I like to end my affirmations with "We are one."

If you do this affirmation at least three times per day, you will begin to see results. Do it before you get out of bed in the morning, mid-day, and immediately before you close your eyes at night. When we insert affirmations into our mind before falling asleep, our amazing Monkey will work on this thought all night! I have journals full of affirmations I have written. Many are expanded versions of these five simple lines, which really say it all for me. If I am working on something specific, I will add some positive reinforcements ("I am strong," "I am healthy," "I am courageous," etc.). The words that follow "I am" are very powerful.

Again, I feel this is a programming language for the Soul. Whatever you call it, affirmations are like freaking magic! You are turning your sights inward and consciously working with Spirit. Human Nature and Divine Nature are now collaborating. I am using my human tools (BBM) to create these affirmations, which reinforce my commitment to Spirit. This is one of the many rewards of Surrender. This is how we communicate with God. What do you have to lose? Give it a try.

I've also created the "I AM" affirmation poster for added inspiration (see page 100). I have one framed in my bedroom, one in my kitchen next to the coffee pot, and one at my office. I read it daily. Our busy lives can drag us away from this state of awareness. These reminders keep me feeling connected. When you start doing this practice regularly, you might want to customize your own affirmations. Mindless repetition of memorized verse can be a waste. I've watched people doing this in church for many years. Some parents can actually smack their kids for misbehaving and never miss a word. Very impressive!

I AM...

BRAVE CHEERFUL ABUNDANT BOLD GRATEFUL LOVED ... COURAGEOUS HEALTHY CONFIDENT JOYOUS GOOD COMPASSION TRUSTWORTHY BRIGHT AUTHENTIC **I AM AWARE** CONFIDENT BLESSED SELFLESS LOVING INFINITE GOD **I AM ONE WITH MY CREATOR** FUN BLISSFUL PASSION STRONG HEROIC JOY **I AM ONE WITH ALL CREATION** FIT BLISS COMPLETE PLAYFUL RELAXED FEARLESS **I AM POWERFUL** THANKFUL RADIANT ENOUGH FUNNY AWESOME **I AM FREE TO EXPRESS MY AUTHENTIC SELF** AWARE GENEROUS BEAUTIFUL LOVE ETERNAL **I AM COURAGEOUS** BLESSED ENTHUSIASTIC ENERGETIC LAUGHTER **I AM ATTRACTING ALL THAT IS NEEDED** ENERGY **FOR MY ADVENTURE** JOYOUS WHOLE INTELLIGENT CARING HAPPY POWERFUL **I AM CREATING** GRATEFUL HEROIC **HEAVEN ON EARTH** STRONG PEACE ABLE SUCCESSFUL LIMITLESS LIGHT PASSIONATE BRILLIANT GRACE

Created by AwareOmLife.com © 2014.

When possible, I like to do my affirmations aloud. I put my hand on my chest and feel the vibration as the words resonate within. In a way, I feel the connection between my Human Nature and Divine Nature through this vibration. If you are willing to take this one step weirder, do these affirmations in the mirror! You might want to lock the bathroom door for this one. When doing mirror work, be enthusiastic, smile, and show some emotion. Eventually, when you look into your eyes, you will begin to feel like you are looking through the mask directly into your Soul. With a wink and a smile, you can acknowledge your connection.

The eyes are the window to the Soul. Every time you look into a mirror, be aware that Body and Soul are now working as a powerful team. With a little practice, this will become a normal part of your day. Louise Hay, founder of Hay House, wrote the book on mirror work, literally. Check out her book entitled *Mirror Work: 21 Days to Heal Your Life*. Remember, one of the biggest rewards of Surrender is communication and collaboration with your Source. This is real. For me, it's as real as sitting down and having a conversation with my wife, but better. Your Spirit doesn't talk back! Hahaha. Sorry. That was a wife joke.

Seriously, Spirit does talk back. When I said the biggest reward of Surrender was our ability to collaborate with

Spirit, I meant this literally. The Universal Mind becomes an extension of your human mind. As you gradually learn how to listen, this will become two-way communication. For those of us who were taught to pray as children and felt this process was always one-sided, your life is about to change. By regularly affirming, "I am a primal man/woman. I am aware of my Divine Nature, I am devoted to You," you will stay connected. Since this was our natural state of being at birth, you will be surprised how easy this is to relearn.

As Super-Man, you will quickly become very in tune with your body. The human body is a magnificent biofeedback instrument. When I need to make a decision about something, I sit quietly for a few minutes and visualize all my options. Listen for your body's feedback during this process. If you feel tense or anxious, this is probably not the correct path. If you feel excited and happy, your inner guide will lead you. If you listen carefully, your body has all the answers. This is intuition in its simplest form. Using the human instrument is one of the many powers Super-Man will develop when he learns to quiet the mind and look within.

At this point, you might be thinking, *wouldn't it be great if God would just talk to me using simple words in my language?* I often wondered this same thing. If you really think about this question, intuition is our primal language.

We didn't come out of the womb understanding English, French, or German. Our language and communication skills have all been learned. Our innate universal language is intuition. Like any language, if you don't use it, you will lose it. With a little effort, we can redevelop this powerful tool. This is how our Divine Nature communicates with our Human Nature.

Intuition is not our only communication method with Spirit. God does speak using words through His many channels. After Surrender, you become more in tune to hear these messages. These channels for expression might be your friends, spouse, children, or even the homeless dude on the street. You will soon discover guidance everywhere. You might also discover a book or spiritual teacher that inspires you. There have been times I have felt a message in a book spoke directly to my Soul. Always keep your focus on the message and not the messenger. Some of my favorite teachers have said, "I am not your guru. Focus on the message, and always look within to find your guru." These teachers are no different from you and me. We are all channels for God's expression. The Universe has many undercover agents.

In addition to the primal language of intuition, and looking for guidance through channels, I also feel we can have *direct* communication with Spirit. When we Surrender, we tap into the Universal Mind.

Consider a computer analogy. What if your computer had no outside data connection? You are unaware this technology even exists. The computer works fine, but you only have access to the data on your local hard drive and the accumulation of past history. One day, someone *flicks a switch* and you have an internet connection. You now have the world at your fingertips. Surrender is equivalent to *flicking the switch*, but this cloud is truly unlimited.

The mind of God now becomes an extension of our human mind. You are no longer limited to the human brain/mind database. We now have access to the unlimited resources of the Universal Mind. I mentioned earlier how your Soul, the eternal part of your being, has been through this process (life) many times. You now get to tap into the accumulated wisdom of the Soul. In addition, being part of this ethereal world, the Soul is our direct-connection with Spirit (God, Source, Creator). So, when I say, "Upon Surrender your Soul will jump for joy," this is why!

The Giant has finally succeeded, completing the merger between Human Nature and Divine Nature. Your poor Monkey Mind, who has been working his ass off trying to protect you for so many years, will also get a break. This powerful computer (mind) will now be taking instructions from the Giant. Let the celebration begin! The results are immediate. A peaceful flow will begin to wash over you. To access this direct communication with Spirit, close your eyes, look within, and ask your questions. Be patient. All the answers will come. This inner dialogue is a skill that will develop over time.

The experience of Surrender is much more than having a personal relationship with the Divine, which is often the promise of many religions. A "relationship" still implies separation. Having this relationship or being aware of the Divine within is not enough. We are actually at this level throughout the Epic Battle. Although this is a good start, because it means you are aware, you are still living in a world of separation. There is still a doer and an observer. There are much higher levels to reach. Yogananda said, "When you discover this flow, it will be like a river running through you. Jump into this river and drown yourself." He means to merge and become one with your Higher Self. This awareness might take a little getting used to, but it's worth the effort. This is your birthright. We are now playing at the highest level of the Game. When these six magic words, "I devote my self to You," become your daily commitment, you will be amazed how life begins to unfold. The second phase of our life's *primal purpose* has been accomplished (Discover-Surrender-Inspire). Human Nature and Divine Nature have finally evolved and merged into one. Surrender is complete.

The reason Surrender feels so good is because you have reconnected with your natural state of being. This is how you were born into this world. You can now transform into Super-Man. Just for the record, this term has nothing to do with the fictional superhero. Again, Super-Man is an abbreviation for supernatural-human. The definition of supernatural is "Godlike." There is nothing fictitious about becoming supernatural. This is part of our evolution on this spiritual path, something that happens when you learn to communicate with your Higher Self. Don't feel self-conscious, undeserving, or embarrassed to use the affirmation, "I am Super-Man." This is your birthright. It's time to reclaim your power!

I resist having this message lumped into what's often called the New Age movement. This is not a New Age concept. In fact, this is actually an age-old message. This is the same message Jesus was teaching 2,000 years ago! I'm not a religious guy, but I found the quotes below to be very powerful.

- *The Father and I are one.* (John 10:30 NLT)
- *Do you not know that you are God's temple and that God's Spirit dwells in you?* (Corinthians 3:16 ESV)
- *Don't you believe that I am in the Father and the Father is in me? The words I say to you I do not speak on my own authority. Rather, it is the Father,*

living in me, doing his work. Whoever believes in me will also do the works that I am doing. (John 14:10 NIV)

I was thrilled to find these quotes since I have long felt that in addition to having the Divine within, each of us are cells in the Body of God. Jesus was not on a mission to start a new religion. Jesus was a spiritual rebel trying to awaken the Sleeping Giant that lies dormant in all of humanity! We are all channels for God's expression. "Whoever believes in me will also do the works that I am doing." It's time to embrace this message and become part of a long-overdue spiritual revolution.

The good news is you can be part of this revolution as a secret agent. Trust me. I know how scary it could be to tell the world how you feel. Do you know how vulnerable I feel right now typing these words, knowing there is a chance someone might read this? Okay, so let's say you are now aware of your secret powers but are not ready to go public. You can choose to be on a covert mission. How cool is that? We need more undercover agents. Post-Surrender, it will become very obvious that you are surrounded by sleepwalkers. This is perfect! You are embedded exactly where you are needed most.

Most people have heard the Gandhi quote, "Be the change that you wish to see in the world." This will be everyone's first step on this covert mission. One of the many rewards of Surrender is that you will start to be kinder to your self. Depending on your lifestyle up to this point, you might experience a panicked feeling in the beginning, as I did. *Oh shit, if I'm hosting God, I'd better get my house in order.* Personally, I was a mess! I was using and abusing drugs and alcohol. My daily routine consisted of smoking, drinking, and eating crap food. I had many bad habits, to say the least. I had spent decades trying to quit these destructive habits but had no willpower. I was always beating myself up for being weak. Willpower is not required after Surrender. You will naturally have the desire to live a healthy lifestyle, to return to your primal way. If I can do it, anyone can!

Luckily for us, the human body is very forgiving. Years of abuse can be quickly reversed. I was amazed how soon my body bounced back to its natural state of health. I must admit it was a little weird at first. I unconsciously started drinking tons of water. I couldn't get enough. I also started to crave fruits and vegetables. I later learned this was the body's natural detox process. It's like flushing the toilet! I didn't need to study any books on the subject. It just began to happen naturally.

If you get out of your own way, you will discover your body already has the answers. I felt the urge to get off the couch and start moving my body (hiking, biking, yoga, etc.). I was also craving nature time, which was very strange for a city boy. I recently listened to an episode of Krista Tippett's *On Being* podcast. Krista interviewed the author Michael McCarthy about his book called *The Moth Snowstorm: Nature and Joy*. Michael explained this mysterious craving.

> For 50,000 generations, we were part of the natural world. We were the wildlife! Just another species wandering the planet. This is where we evolved, learned our instincts, learned how to feel, and react. This is where our imaginations formed. This bond with nature is very deep in our tissue. It has only been the last five hundred generations, since the development of farming, that we have been removed. We might have left the natural world, but the natural world has not left us.

This explains a lot! Nature is baked into our DNA. It is very unnatural for us to be living in these concrete jungles, spending our days surrounded by artificial light, and the hum of electronics. As human beings, we have forgotten our connection to the natural world. We don't even know that we are going through withdrawal. We just know something feels off. As a civilization, we are becoming more depressed, anxious, and lethargic, but we don't know why. For me, discovering the remedy was accidental. I began to hike, bike, and trail run for exercise. I discovered my hours spent in the forest instantly lifted my mood. I now plan my days to include this nature fix.

These life changes should not be considered a new diet or exercise routine. We are simply returning to our primal way. We need to take off our shoes and get dirty! We need to move our asses every day! Bodies in motion stay healthy by burning the calories we consume each day. Food is fuel. We need to burn as much as we consume. This isn't rocket science. The quality of our fuel is also important. We wouldn't think of putting cheap fuel into the tanks of our precious cars, but we routinely poison our bodies. We need to stop playing dumb! We all know what is healthy and what is not. Turn off the TV. Don't fall for the brainwashing! With a little effort, this healthy lifestyle will become natural. You will quickly begin to see positive changes in your body, emotions, and attitudes. These positive results will be all the inspiration you need. You will notice how these changes affect the people around you. Remember, we are on a covert mission. Be the change. We need to lead by example, and this is the first step. Know that when you begin to make these changes, those around you are watching.

In addition to the primal instinct of being kind to yourself, you will also become nicer to those around you. In this new post-Surrender world, you become more aware of your connection to others. You have not only discovered your own Divine Nature, but you also intuitively see the Divine in all. You will become an uplifting force in your family, workplace, and community. Again, this all happens naturally. You will soon discover this *primal way* feels really good.

During the process of writing this book, I find myself continuously drawn to this concept of a *Primal Way*. The word *primal* is derived from *primordial,* which means "the original stage of an organism's development." This underlying theme became very obvious: primal fear, primal purpose, primal language, primal instinct, primal life, etc. I apologize for the repetition, but this word perfectly reflects what I am describing. I often say, "I'm not a religious guy," but maybe this *Primal Way* is my religion. After all, what is the definition of religion? Isn't it a set of beliefs we use as a foundation for our lives?

When I researched the word *religion*, I discovered the Latin root *religare* actually means "to bind or reconnect." This idea of reconnection is at the core of what I'm calling our Primal Way. I discovered the same concept when researching the meaning of the word *yoga*. In the Vedas, the world's oldest scriptures, yoga is defined as "union." *It is the practice of uniting Body, Soul and Spirit.* Holy crap! Everywhere I dig reveals the same treasure! Can the spiritual path really be this simple? The answer is yes. All paths lead to this one truth, one song, or universe. This is the common denominator that connects all religions. It is literally the definition of the word *religion*. The purpose of life is to Discover and Surrender to the Divine within (reconnect/unite). What a loving and peaceful world this would be if we could all focus on what unites us. I believe this Primal Way can supercharge any traditional religious practice or be used as a religion of its own.

The next stage of this journey is to Inspire others on this path. Our heroic mission is to be the spark that awakens the Giant in all. You now have the power and the energy to do this. These are the early stages of Super-Man's development. Slowly but surely, you will begin to see people around you changing. Leading by example is a powerful tool. Just think what would happen if we had millions of undercover agents on this planet leading by example!

As I read the news throughout the day, it often feels like the world is going crazy. I've never really been into politics, but a revolution is long overdue. Again, we start small by following Gandhi's "Be the change" philosophy. This leads to changes in our families and communities. These grassroots community movements can grow to inspire changes on a national and global level.

If enough like-minded people join together, change can be relatively quick. Have you heard of *the power of the pocketbook?* We have the power to choose where we spend our money, or more importantly, where we don't spend our money! Being conscious consumers can force large corporations to act more responsibly. This is happening now. John Mackey, founder of Whole Foods, has been a leader in the *conscious capitalism* movement. When John was interviewed by Oprah on *SuperSoul Conversations*, he said, "Love has been in the closet for too long in corporate America. Conscious entrepreneurs will change the world." What does this mean? In a nutshell, corporations are not necessarily evil. A new wave of conscious leaders is driving this revolution. These leaders understand that business is a voluntary exchange of goods and services. In order to create a long-lasting successful business model, we must authentically care about *all* stakeholders. This includes our customers, employees, suppliers, the community, and the environment.

Everything is interconnected. The old-school model of business as a machine whose only purpose was to generate profit will no longer work in this new world. Again, we have the power to choose where we spend our money. Conscious consumers will help drive this revolution.

We also need to get organized and vote together. There is power in numbers. As we progress along our spiritual path, we will begin to see our leaders in a new light. Our bullshit detector becomes very sensitive. We will begin to demand more. Although I mention organizing with "like-minded" people, it is critical that we do not lose our civility in the process. The Institute for Civility in Government defines civility as follows:

> Claiming and caring for one's identity, needs, and beliefs without degrading someone else's in the process. It's about disagreeing without disrespecting. To seek common ground as a starting point for dialogue about our differences. Civility is the hard work of staying present even when we have deep-rooted and fierce disagreements.

If our only common ground for organizing is hate toward the opposition, this downward spiral will never end. It often feels like we have forgotten the values this country was founded on. You don't need to become an activist, but at a minimum, we all need to get out and vote! The small percentage of Americans who actually exercise their civic duty is embarrassing. If you don't like what you see, let your voice be heard.

I believe this Trump era will prove to be a blessing in disguise. Everything happens for a reason! It has become a wake-up call to the world! Brené Brown, in her book *Braving the Wilderness,* discusses the power of "collective joy" and "collective pain." She explains that during these highly emotional states, we feel a sense of connection to our fellow man. Like Brené, I've lived in Houston for many years. We've directly experienced this theory many times in our hometown. For example, I have witnessed the *collective pain* brought on by some devastating hurricanes. Nothing seems to bring people together more than a natural disaster. Brené said, "When the rescue boat pulls up to your house, they don't ask who you voted for." I believe this connection is a primal instinct. It's in our DNA.

On the flip side, I took my son to the World Series when the Houston Astros won in 2017. The *collective joy* felt on the streets was amazing! It was like one big group hug! It didn't matter if you were young, old, rich, poor, black, or white. Unfortunately, it often takes these dramatic highs and lows to activate these instincts. Maybe the turmoil created by this political era we are now experiencing will trigger our primal instinct to come together for a common good. I already see this shift happening. People are starting to get energized and organized, taking a stand against fearmongering and hate. This slow downward spiral started long before Trump, but maybe this is exactly what was needed to speed up the process and begin our recovery! Remember, no mistakes.

I know you are probably sick of me talking about all the rewards associated with Surrender, but there is none better than knowing you are safe and secure in the arms of your Creator. Anxiety, fear, and worry begin to melt away. You can finally relax and enjoy the natural flow of life. I can now see how all experiences have been for my benefit, leading me to this moment.

Now that you are listening to guidance from within, you will naturally make fewer mistakes. Life literally becomes easier. You begin to listen to your intuition and good results follow. You build a new foundation based on these positive results. You begin to gain confidence and faith. Don't get me wrong. You will still make some mistakes and bad stuff can still happen, but it's different. You are coming from this peaceful place where you feel secure and protected. Your intentions are good, and you don't need to live in fear anymore.

It is time to remember that we were born into royalty. You are the son/daughter of the King. Do you understand now why it was necessary to forget? If we were aware of our Divine Nature throughout the early stages of development, we would have never voluntarily gone into the darkness to learn the lessons needed to strengthen us in preparation for this heroic mission. To be effective leaders, we needed to experience all stages of life in order to have empathy and understanding for those who are suffering. We are now ready to return to our tribe and inspire others on this path. We fought against life for so long that sometimes *being in the flow* feels too good to be true. God doesn't grant access to these powers until he knows you are ready, and Surrender was the next step.

Surrender represents the reunion of Body, Soul, and Spirit. The Soul has successfully completed its mission to reunite Body and Spirit. The Giant had to become a master negotiator to facilitate the most important merger humanity will ever know. This is the purpose of creation. This is the Game of Life.

For those who are wondering, the story does not end here. No, we don't Surrender and disappear into a puff of smoke. The final stage of this Game is magical! This new awareness has transformed the Body and Soul into Super-Man.

SUMMARY

This chapter was all about our powerful Human Nature finally surrendering to the Divine within. The Bodyguard found the courage to be vulnerable and hand over the controls to the Giant. It is time to move from surviving to thriving. Body and Soul have reconnected. To be more accurate, they were never really separate. This reunion occurs when the *illusion of separation* is exposed.

Surrender represents fulfilling part two of our Primal Purpose (Discover-Surrender-Inspire). A daily meditation practice is essential to keep the line of communication open with our Source. This conscious communication is one of the many rewards of Surrender. In addition to meditation, using affirmations is a great way to collaborate with the Soul. Start practicing these communication skills now. Don't waste another day! Like any new language, there is a learning curve. We will need to be fluent to excel in the next stage of this amazing journey.

CHAPTER 5

INSPIRE

The final stage on this journey is to live out your life as Super-Man, inspiring others on this path. Since this is an inside job, your friends and family might not even notice a difference. Sorry, no bulging muscles. No halo will appear over your head.

This is all part of the Game Plan. You can now begin to work covertly on your mission, embedded among the sleepwalkers. If I had any regrets, it would be wishing I had reached this stage sooner. This is why I have spent so much time examining why we resist Surrender. During the process of writing this book, I figured out that I reached the Discovery stage when I was about thirty years old. Unfortunately, I wasn't ready for Surrender until I was fifty-two. That's embarrassing! I must remind myself, no mistakes. I obviously still had many lessons to learn.

When the dust settles after the long Epic Battle, we discover a new being has risen from the ashes. I believe Spirit has been patiently waiting for this moment. If life is a Game, the name of the game would be *Evolution*. How long will it take for Body and Soul to evolve and become Super-Man?

The many rewards of Surrender that I have revealed throughout this book are immediate. They might be subtle at first, so pay close attention. These positive results will quickly reinforce your decision to Surrender. All changes in life have a learning curve. The more skilled you become at following your inner guidance, the easier life will flow. We talked about being *in the zone* and the possibility of living in this state full time. This is what we are working toward. The pain, suffering, and struggles previously associated with life begin to melt away. When you are *in the zone,* it starts to feel like life is stacked in your favor, because it is!

As Super-Man, knowing you are hosting God on this brief earthly adventure, you will naturally feel the urge to keep your house in order. With this goal in mind, you need to be strong, healthy, and full of energy. If you're going to be a vehicle for God's expression, why not be a freaking Ferrari!

If our mission is to attract and inspire others on this path, we need to lead by example! Remember, our Bodyguard has relinquished control. With the Giant back in charge, this becomes an easy natural process. Destructive habits and addictions will begin to melt away. We didn't come into this world needing all this external crap to be okay. You will naturally move toward a life centered on wellness. This process was not a struggle like it was in the past when my motivations were ego driven.

Most spiritual teachings focus exclusively on the Spirit and Soul, vilifying the role of the Body. I believe the Body is equally important in any spiritual discussion and possibly the most important piece of the puzzle. As I have said many times, the *purpose of creation* is evolution of the Soul. The Soul cannot evolve without a Body! Although the Soul is eternal and will get many return trips if necessary, the Body only gets one try! If we are lucky enough to discover the Sleeping Giant and courageous enough to Surrender, we have earned the right to play this Game at the highest level.

I believe this spiritual path is meant to be fun. The fun doesn't really begin until after Surrender. I believe many seekers get stuck because they fall into the trap of thinking this path is meant to be very somber, serious, and full of sacrifice. OMG! Nothing can be further from the truth! This is a lighthearted path that is full of joy, laughter, and abundance. When free from attachment, we can enjoy the abundance the world has to offer. When you hear someone say, "Life's a bitch and then you die," they have not yet discovered the truth. I am grateful for making it to this level of the Game. In a way, I feel like the veil has been lifted and some secrets have been revealed. I can only hope that by sharing some of my discoveries, I might speed up this process for others. As I mentioned in the beginning, my motivation for writing this book was to share these discoveries with my kids. I'm hoping they won't be as stubborn as their dad.

Speaking of kids, we need more young people to join this spiritual revolution. The sooner they can get from Discovery to Surrender the better! They will be our future leaders. This is how all revolutions begin. Like-minded people come together and decide it is time for change. If we are successful at inspiring young people, some of these "awakened" young adults might become community leaders or run for political office. Our world will quickly change when our leaders know the secret. What will happen when this enlightened generation begins to have children? As super-parents, their children will be raised to understand these Universal Truths. This new generation will carry on the spiritual revolution we are starting today!

Regardless of the love and awareness coming from these super-parents, we all must leave the nest. Everyone must experience Human Nature and its many lessons. Primal fear, the creation of the Bodyguard, and the School of Life cannot be avoided. However, maybe with super-parents, these children will have this awareness at a younger age and their Bodyguards won't need to be as strong or stubborn.

As we now know, after Surrender, we start to become kinder to ourselves and others. We have love and respect for all living things, including the planet. Wow! How awesome would it be to have this awareness as a child! How different would the world look today? This is not some crazy dream. This could happen very soon! With a little help and some luck, this message can go viral. Why not? Do you see how fast negative messages and fake news are spread across the planet via Twitter, Instagram, Facebook, and other social media platforms? Someone posts a video or a tweet and within minutes the world is buzzing about it. Maybe we can use this technology to our advantage. Can a positive message go viral? Oprah, we need your help! We are long overdue for this spiritual revolution. We need to awaken the Sleeping Giant in all and reclaim our power! Unfortunately, most of us won't Surrender until old age, if ever. It's up to us lucky few to share this awareness and Inspire others. This is Super-Man's mission. This is the final step of our collective primal purpose as human beings.

As you've probably figured out by now, Wayne Dyer was a big inspiration when I first became a seeker. Dr. Dyer spent most of his life inspiring others on this path. Wayne wrote thirty-eight books, including the children's book *I Am: Why Two Little Words Mean so Much*. This book teaches the simple but profound message that you are not separate from God. If you have kids or know anyone with children, buy them this book. You will instantly become an active participant in this revolution.

Step out of the shadows and become a rebel. If you are met with resistance, don't be discouraged. You are surrounded by sleepwalkers. Don't give up!

Let me give you an example of some resistance related to this message. In 2012, my son was in a leadership program called PALs (Peer Assistance Leadership) at his high school. This is a great organization, providing a valuable service to the community. In a nutshell, PAL is all about kids helping kids. Students participating in the program help younger at-risk kids as mentors. Anyway, being the naive guy that I am, I purchased two hundred copies of Wayne's children's book to donate to this program. Hay House was kind enough to add fifty free books to my purchase (250 books total). To my surprise, the donation was rejected by the program director. When I asked why, I was told, "Because this book teaches children that God is inside of them." Wow! I was shocked. I thought this was a fantastic message that might help troubled kids improve their self-image and confidence. To make a long story short, I found another organization happy to accept this donation, and I learned a valuable lesson along the way. Not everyone is ready for this message, but do not be discouraged.

While doing research for this chapter, I discovered that my description of the spiritual path is very similar to what Joseph Campbell called the "Hero's Journey." Campbell explains that throughout history, our mythology and folklore have followed a common theme or template. He describes a hero who "ventures from the common world into a world of supernatural wonder." The hero encounters many challenges along this journey. After claiming victory over his demons, the hero is transformed. In the final step of this journey, the hero "returns to the ordinary world with the wisdom he has gained, which he may now use for the benefit of his fellow man."

Campbell feels this recurring story shows a unity of humanity's spiritual history. He calls it "the story behind the story." This hero's journey can be seen in the life of Buddha, Moses, and Jesus. The template can also be seen in many popular movies, such as *The Wizard of Oz*, *The Matrix*, *The Hunger Games*, *Star Wars*, *Lord of the Rings*, and *The Lion King*. What fascinates me is that this theme is naturally recurring. In other words, Buddha was not trying to copy Moses. Ancient myths originating on opposite ends of the planet *naturally* followed this common theme.

What's the big deal? When something naturally repeats for the history of civilization, it should be considered a Universal Truth. I believe the spiritual journey that I am describing in this book (Birth, School of Life, Discovery, Epic Battle, Surrender, and Inspire) also falls into this category. Why does this story continue to repeat itself?

Because there really is only *one truth,* and no religion can claim it. Once we remember this Universal Truth, as Campbell says, "It's time to return to the ordinary world with the wisdom we have gained, which may now be used for the benefit of all." We will have a natural desire to inspire others on this path.

Upon Surrender, the sky will not open and suck you up into the heavens. As awesome as that would be, we still have work to do. You will naturally feel a strong desire to serve. You will lead by example and inspire others. This is the third and final stage of our collective primal purpose as human beings. Joseph Benner describes this stage beautifully in his book *Christ in You.*

> Love must pour itself out. A longing came to me to help those who were coming along the road I had traveled. Oh, to tell them something of the indwelling Christ. We love you all and long to show you what you possess.

This is it! This is Super-Man's heroic mission. If you are one of the lucky ones who have made it this far, don't stop now! We will have a natural "longing" to inspire others on this journey.

Those *six magic words* I discussed in the previous chapter, *I devote my self to You,* which were originally my commitment for Surrender, have now become a call to action. As I continued using these magical words as part of my daily affirmation practice, I began to hear this response: "Okay, show me what you've got!" This reply was a pleasant surprise. I looked at this as a friendly challenge from the Universe. Enough talk! It's time for some action. This call to action was another type of awakening for me. I started to wonder, *What do I have to offer?* You see, upon Surrender, no one will be turned away. However, the Universe will never dish out more than you can handle. Human Nature and Divine Nature are equal partners on this adventure. I want this experience to be *big*. I want to proclaim, "I am ready. Choose me. I can handle it!" What might have been difficult as an unconscious sleepwalker has now become easy.

You will find this urge to be strong and healthy is a natural post-Surrender experience. I added these commitments to my daily affirmations as a response to the challenge:

> I am a strong, powerful man.
> I am healthy, wealthy, and wise.
> I am confident and courageous.
> I am leading by example.

Remember, I strongly recommend you write your own affirmations. We all know our personal weak spots, and this is a powerful tool for growth. These affirmations are your direct communication with Spirit, who is always listening to your sincere desires. If these statements are not true in this moment, they soon will be.

How do we attract and inspire others on this heroic mission? You will discover a creative life-force now flows through you. All obstacles will be removed. There will be a natural energy shift within. I am not referring to a caffeine-like energy but to a high vibration in every cell of your body. You might not feel a difference at first, but those around you will notice. In other words, your energy will have a positive effect on others. I am sure everyone has experienced this phenomenon at one time or another. You are in a public place (bank, store, coffee shop, etc.) and someone walks through the door radiating a positive feel-good energy. It's hard to explain, but you can feel an energy shift in the room. Their presence makes everyone around them feel good. Without saying a word, your new awareness has made you a channel for God's expression. It's a mystical, magical thing that starts to happen. You will find this energy now flows naturally through you. Get used to it.

Obviously, this first example was very passive. Another method is to simply make eye contact and share a friendly smile with everyone you encounter during your day. If you want to take it to the next level, share a kind word.

You will be amazed how powerful a smile and a few words can be. You won't need to force yourself to do this. After some initial awkwardness, this too will become natural.

The next method of influence is a little more active. We can all *lead by example*. Again, be aware others are watching you at all times, especially when they notice you changing. This gives us a great opportunity to inspire. How you speak and interact with others will begin to shift. For example, if you've always been a hard-ass personality type, you will begin to soften. If you are quiet or shy, you begin to open up. If you have been rushing through life, too busy for other people, you will naturally slow down. Buddhism refers to this as "The Middle Way," which describes moderation between extremes. This too is effortless. You will begin to *feel* a connection with life. You will look for opportunities to help those close to you. This is not exclusively for your fellow humans but also toward the planet and all living things. Don't panic. I'm not expecting this shift to turn everyone into composting vegetarians who drive electric cars, but we will naturally begin to make more conscious decisions, feeling our connection to all of creation.

The next development on Super-Man's journey will be an urge to contribute to the world. I am not necessarily talking about money, although if you've got some extra bucks to share, there are many great organizations in need of financial support. Unlike the previous methods, this phase of your heroic mission does take some effort. This is where we get to be creative. The recurring question should not be "What's my purpose?" Since we all share the same purpose, a better question would be, "How shall I serve?"

This is when personal preference comes into play. We get to break free from the pack and choose our own path. This should be fun! Just because Human Nature and Divine Nature have reunited doesn't mean you've become a robot. You have been given an amazing body, brain, mind, personality, and ego. Yes, even the ego! When the Bodyguard surrenders, the ego happily becomes a humble servant of the Soul. This is when we get to show our individuality! Yogananda says, "This purified ego merges with Soul and becomes our individual reflection of God on earth."

What do you feel drawn toward? I promise you will feel a pull to do something. Do you like working with children, the elderly, or the homeless? Are you drawn to social causes or environmental issues? Although I say this takes some effort, you will not need to force yourself to do this. If it does not feel natural, it's not the right channel. When I reached this point in my journey, opportunities *coincidentally* started to show up everywhere. I can give you a few examples of organizations I've discovered that have turned into amazing experiences.

- water.org. This organization is helping people globally by providing resources for water and sanitation solutions. This has proven to be very empowering for women in these communities, who have traditionally been responsible for collecting water for their families. The simple act of finding and retrieving water not only consumes many hours per day but can also put these women into dangerous situations. Over the past twenty-five years, water.org has helped more than sixteen million people gain access to safe water. If you purchased this e-book, you have already begun your heroic mission. 100% of proceeds are donated to this great cause.

- www.safeaustin.org. Safe Place Austin is an amazing women's shelter in Texas offering tons of services to women in need. Some of the services include safe shelter, child care, education, job assistance, medical, legal assistance, and counseling. Their *Expect Respect* program helps educate young girls on building healthy relationships and preventing violence and abuse.

- www.met-min.org. For nearly four decades, MetMin has been helping individuals and families in crisis by helping with emergency financial assistance combined with services to keep the crisis from recurring. Help with rent, utilities, and food are the first step. MetMin's mission is to stop homelessness before it starts.

- www.danshouseofhope.org. Dan's House of Hope helps young adults fighting cancer heal through community, supportive programming, and home-away-from-home services that reduce isolation, decrease financial burdens, and nourish hope.

- www.periwinklefoundation.org. Since the Periwinkle Foundation's inception in 1983, pediatric oncologists have made great strides in improving the overall cure rate of children with cancer. Nearly 80 percent of children diagnosed with cancer now survive. While more children are surviving, successful treatment may leave them with mental or physical complications that can impact them for the rest of their lives. Periwinkle Programs play a vital role in the overall healing process of these special children, teens, and families by providing camps and other life-changing programs.

- Vote.org. This organization uses technology to simplify political engagement, increase voter turnout, and strengthen American democracy. This is accomplished by maintaining an extensive website with information on voting deadlines, voter ID requirements, early voting, absentee ballots, and links to resources for all fifty states. In addition, Vote.org contacts potential voters to encourage them to register and vote!

I mention these organizations for some real-life examples of opportunities to serve both locally and globally. If you have not been involved with any kind of service work yet, you will soon discover why I call this an "amazing experience." In the beginning, I actually felt a little guilty since it made *me* feel so good! This is truly a trifecta of goodness. First and most important, you get to help those in need. Second, you are leading by example and inspiring others on this path. Third, you discover how amazing it makes you feel.

Finally, some day you may decide to remove your mask and take your heroic mission public. Although this step is not necessary to play this Game at its highest level, you might be able to have a bigger impact. Those choosing to go public might be inspired to create a nonprofit, start a blog, or become an activist. There is no ranking system when it comes to service. It's all good. You decide how you want to express yourself. You are the writer, director, and lead actor in your adventure. When I say the spiritual path is supposed to be fun, this is what I'm talking about! You are now co-creating. You are a channel for God's expression. You will be amazed how your life will begin to change. The best is yet to come.

To better understand the creation of Super-Man and our journey into the "supernatural world of wonder," as Joseph Campbell called it, I will summarize the evolution of Body and Soul as I see it. I apologize for the constant repetition on this subject, but this is very, very important stuff. Without this understanding, you cannot advance.

THE JOURNEY OF THE SOUL

God's purpose for creation is evolution of the Soul. The Soul cannot evolve without a Body. Yes, you are important! Don't let anyone tell you otherwise. Every Body is born with a Soul. Will the Soul awaken and learn to commune with its mortal self? Can we get in sync, surrender, and merge? How does this journey end? Does the Soul return empty-handed, or do we end this adventure as Super-Man? This is God's *Game of Life*.

THE JOURNEY OF THE BODY

Man's purpose is to Discover, Surrender and Inspire. How long will it take man to discover the Sleeping Giant within? How long will the Giant and the Bodyguard battle before Surrender? After Surrender, will we become leaders and inspire others on this path? This too is God's

Game of Life. If you are one of the lucky few to reach this level of the Game, you become a Super-Man! This is when the magic begins. Hopefully, we will all reach this stage with plenty of time left to play.

Have you noticed the common denominator in these two stories? Man's purpose and God's purpose are one in the same. The quest to become Super-Man is *the* end game.

SUMMARY

When the dust settled from our long Epic Battle, we discovered a new being had risen from the ashes. The final stage of this journey is to live out your life as Super-Man, inspiring others on this adventure. We will soon find the entire Universe conspires to help us on our mission. This path was meant to be lighthearted and fun. In this final stage, we discover the authentic joy associated with being part of this spiritual revolution. The time is now. Don't waste another moment. Be the change and inspire others.

THE END

THE RABBIT HOLE

If you are curious and would like to go further down the rabbit hole, I am including a list of resources (books, authors, podcasts, etc.) that have inspired me on this journey.

BOOKS

- Joseph Benner: *Christ in You* and *The Impersonal Life*
- Brené Brown: *Daring Greatly* and *Braving the Wilderness*
- Joseph Campbell: *The Hero's Journey*
- Joe Dispenza: *Becoming Supernatural* and *You Are the Placebo*
- Wayne Dyer: *Your Sacred Self, Real Magic* and *The Shift*
- Annie Grace: *This Naked Mind*
- Louise Hay: *Mirror Work: 21 Days to Heal Your Life*
- Carl Jung: *The Stages of Life*
- John Mackey: *Conscious Capitalism*

- Michael McCarthy: *The Moth Snowstorm: Nature and Joy*
- Anita Moorjani: *Dying to Be Me*
- Michael Singer: *The Untethered Soul* and *The Surrender Experiment*
- Paramahansa Yogananda: *The Autobiography of a Yogi*, *The Second Coming of Christ*, and *God Talks with Arjuna: The Bhagavad Gita*

PODCASTS

- Oprah's SuperSoul Conversations: Awaken, discover, and connect to the deeper meaning of the world around you. Listen to interviews with thought leaders, authors, and spiritual luminaries, as well as health and wellness experts. Designed to guide you through life's big questions. *oprah.com/supersoul*
- On Being: Hosted by Krista Tippett, this podcast examines "the animating questions at the center of human life and what it means to be human." Krista tackles these big questions with scientists, authors, theologians, artists, and teachers from around the globe. *onbeing.org*
- Optimize: This podcast is hosted by Brian Johnson, who boils down "big ideas" from self-development, spiritual and philosophical

literature. Brian has dedicated himself to distilling the world's wisdom into a framework we can all apply to our daily lives. *optimize.me*

MISCELLANEOUS

- Michael Singer's website is a great resource for his books, lectures, interviews, podcasts, and much more. Visit www.untetheredsoul.com.
- *Finding Joe* is a film about Joseph Campbell's *Hero's Journey*. Go to www.findingjoethemovie.com to learn more.
- Elaine Christine is a Life Coach and owner of *Yoga for You* studio in Austin, Tx. Visit www.yogaforyouaustin.com for more info.
- Nate Jensen is an award-winning freelance artist based in Portland, OR. Nate's illustrations in this book helped bring life and humor to my story. For more info, visit www.natepjensen.com.

AwesOm Life

Thank you for reading my book. I strongly believe that if enough like-minded people join together with positive intentions, we can change the world. The formula for this spiritual revolution is simple: ***Be the change and inspire others.*** If this message resonates with you, please share the link to this book. Since 100% of eBook proceeds benefit water.org, you will automatically become an undercover agent on this heroic mission. Enlist in the AwesOm Army today and begin receiving our monthly newsletter and blog.

Namaste,

Craig

www.awesomlife.com

www.awesomlife.com/book

www.awesomlife.com/enlist

AHA MOMENTS

AHA MOMENTS

Made in the USA
Columbia, SC
04 May 2021